Rolf Boldrewood

**The Miner's Right**

A tale of the Australian goldfields. Vol. 2

Rolf Boldrewood

**The Miner's Right**
*A tale of the Australian goldfields. Vol. 2*

ISBN/EAN: 9783337318949

Printed in Europe, USA, Canada, Australia, Japan

Cover: Foto ©Suzi / pixelio.de

More available books at **www.hansebooks.com**

# A TALE OF
# THE AUSTRALIAN GOLDFIELDS

BY

## ROLF BOLDREWOOD

AUTHOR OF 'ROBBERY UNDER ARMS'

IN THREE VOLUMES

VOL. II

London

## MACMILLAN AND CO

AND NEW YORK

1890

# THE MINER'S RIGHT

## CHAPTER XIII

TIME, which brings all things to an end, and which had never passed so slowly for us before, even in our worst 'tucker' days, brought on the hearing of our appeal. It was heard before four magistrates in petty sessions assembled; 'and the whole weary evidence taken over again without the omission of a single detail. It certainly was a fact that Cyrus Yorke's being now the proud possessor of a Miner's Right led the opposite side to dwell with less persistent energy upon that point. But on the other hand they devoted the whole strength of their resources to bring out in strong relief their other allegation, viz. that the irregularity of the shape of our claim constituted a fatal objection.

An appeal lay to two or more magistrates under the Goldfields Act of 30 Victoria, No. 8 (long since repealed), and was not so much an appeal upon certain clearly defined points of law as a total rehearing of the whole case at issue. Hence the defeated party, generally being shrewd enough to discover the weak point of their evidence the first trial, not unfrequently took measures to strengthen that precise gabion or outwork when the appeal was heard. No doubt in some parts of the land the magistrates of the territory, not familiarly acquainted with mining law, constituted a wholly unsatisfactory tribunal before which to decide such delicate details and complicated issues. But the Justices at Yatala had been so thoroughly trained by a long series of mining cases and appeals during years past, involving vast sums and most important consequences, that the more important personages of the higher courts were hardly better up in the rule of evidence and the statutory necessities of their position.

So the whole lengthy evidence was fully and patiently heard; no detail was omitted; the irregular shape of the claim, and the number of superficial feet which it measured, must have been as well known to the habitues of the Court as a catch sum in arithmetic to the boys of a public school at examination time.

At nightfall the magistrates retired to confer among themselves; and after a quarter of an hour's council delivered their decision by the mouth of the chairman. The appeal was dismissed with seventy-five pounds costs against the appellants.

All recourse had now been exhausted but one. Of that one, however, our antagonists were determined to avail themselves.

Furious at defeat, and with a few sarcastic sentences reflecting upon the legal capacity of the magistrates, for which he was promptly called to order, the Doctor at once hurled his last challenge at our heads in the form of a notice of appeal to the Supreme Court.

He was informed that he could do so in the manner set forth in the regulations, by naming the points upon which he desired to appeal, and by lodging a sum of money as guarantee for the costs of the respondents in the event of the appeal being dismissed.

Money was still forthcoming, it appeared, as these expensive preliminaries were at once complied with.

Thus for the second time we were victorious. As we left the Court amid the congratulations of the crowd, Mr. Markham cheerfully asked the Doctor if he had made arrangements for sending the case home to the Privy Council after the Supreme Court had decided against him.

Frowning darkly, he replied that 'it was not so very certain that he might *not* be compelled to take that step also. He had had reason to distrust the law of colonial judges before now.'

Here the crowd cheered him, evidently pleased with his indomitable courage. And we went straight to our claim, and put on a shift before midnight.

A week at least must elapse before the judge in chambers—in his metropolitan seclusion—could be moved to grant an injunction to further restrain us from working until the last appeal should be tried. We therefore concluded to make hay while the sun shone, or rather to dig gold while the coast was clear. To that end we put on a crowd of wages-men, who extracted such a ceaseless output of wash-dirt that our foes used to come to the claim and declare that nothing would be left of their inheritance, so to speak, if we were not stopped.

The Doctor tried the Commissioner and the magistrates for a restraining order, offering to make affidavit that bloodshed would ensue. But the former said if a few rascally, loafing jumpers were knocked on the head it would matter little. And the other men in authority had doubts as to the legality of any but judicial interference at this stage of proceedings.

One fine day, though, an imposing document, with the judge's sign-manual appended thereto, did make its appearance, and was duly served upon us; but before it arrived we had washed several machines of dirt, and extracted the best part of two thousand pounds in hard cash from the 'mining tenement' in dispute.

'Yon dirt goes better and better every load,' said Joe Bulder. 'Danged if I don't chuck that Doctor down a wet shaft if we're muddled about much langer a' this fashion.'

There was nothing for it, however, but to sling up the raw-hide buckets, and put No. 4 out of commission once more. It was hard, too, to see even other claims along the lead, with their red flags flaunting in the breeze, and the whip-horses hauling steadily at their ascending loads, or trolling back briskly and kicking playfully when the descending rope permitted such gambols.

We had, perforce, to endure more wearisome monotonous inaction and delay. Our appeal case in the Supreme Court was set down for hearing at the end of a crowded session, as luck would have it, and immediately before the long vacation. Australian judges are, as a rule, worked very hard, and have not the leisure of their European brethren. At this particular time the course of litigation, consequent upon an unprecedented period of inflowing wealth, had well-nigh exhausted the metropolitan bench, the bar, and even the sufficiently numerous solicitors. Two or three stupendous squatting actions, notably the great Terri-hi-hi Creek case, had swallowed up the last remnant of that admittable patience and attention to minutest details which so honourably distinguishes the British wearer of the ermine.

To the passionate grief and indignation of Dr. Bellair, who stopped but little short of a threat of impeachment before the British Houses of Parliament, the great appeal case in Pole and party *v.* Ingerstrom and party, which was beginning to be in all men's mouths, the value of the claim in dispute being variously stated from a hundred thousand pounds to a quarter of a million, was not brought on before the close of the session.

So it was left stranded with other forlorn argosies, and compelled to abide the humble position of remanet.

We were hardly less disgusted than our enthusiastic opponent that his frantic adjurations had beaten themselves vainly against the rock of judicial imperturbability. Whatever were we to do for the three or four, possibly six, months which would probably intervene before we could put a pick again into the tantalisingly rich wash-dirt of No. 4? How were we to spend our money or our lives in this confounded Yatala, thrice-read volume that it was to all of us?

Events follow quickly in those new lands

upon which the Southern Cross looks down
from the untroubled skies, fortunately for those
sons of hazard and adventure, for whom the
measured march of the old world has ever been
too tame.    I had wandered listlessly homeward one evening from a long day's walk, more
than usually depressed with the thought that
the waters of evil fortune were closing darkly
over our heads in spite of our transient gold
gleam, when I was struck by the unwonted
appearance of activity displayed by the Major.

Our premises also had undergone a temporary alteration.    The tent was down ; various
articles of furniture were assuming their well-
known travelling appearance.    Joe Bulder was
briskly busied in abetting the transformation of
everything into light marching order.    Suddenly I became conscious of an unwonted hum
as of earnest voices amongst our circumjacent
acquaintances.    I began to recognise the symp-
toms of the complaint.

It was not for the first time that I had known
a great goldfield infected by it.    Forms were
flitting about in the gathering twilight, lanterns
were being lit in preparation for night work.
Horses were driven up, the hobble chains and

bells of which sounded their continuous characteristic chime.    A word from time to time
caught my ear, in which 'The Oxley,' 'Only a
hundred and odd miles,' 'Five ounces to the
dish,' 'Good sinking,' All block claims,' were
increasingly distinct.

Before I stopped at the spot of earth which
had been immediately before our own tent door,
I was fully aware of the cause of the unwonted
agitation which characterised the night.

A rush was on, and a big one at that, as I
heard an American digger inform his mate.

'You're a good fellow, Pole,' said the Major,
'in your way—a man of high principles and
irreproachable morals ; but these infernally long
walks amount to a defect in your character.
Here have we been sounding boot and saddle
all day, and couldn't get "tale or tidings of you,"
as Mrs. Yorke says.    Lend a hand with this
cord.    Do you want to put anything else in this
box of yours ?    I've packed it for you.'

'I'll see in the morning,' I said.    'Where's
the rush ?'

'*Where's* the rush ?' echoed the Major, still
tugging away at an obstinate cord with which
he was securing a very bulging and battered

portmanteau. 'Have you been in a cave all day? or where in heaven can you have deposited yourself not to have heard of the Great Rush to the Oxley—the biggest thing that's happened in Australia yet, and that's going to knock Ballarat and Bendigo into a cocked hat?'

'So good as that?' I queried languidly.

'Good!' shouted the Major. '*Nothing* ever heard like it, even in California or Eaglehawk. Three ounces, five ounces, ten ounces to the dish, regular chunks of gold, no rock, no water. All shallow sinking and block claims; none of your confounded frontage, all law and humbug. I like the good old-fashioned blocks—when you get it, you get it and no mistake. There won't be a soul on the field in a week, except those who are on real good gold. And it *must* be good to keep fellows here after what we've heard.'

'How about No. 4; give it away?'

'No, most noble stoic, we are not exactly going to do that, badly as we have been treated by luck, law, and litigation. You and I and Joe are going "right away," as poor Gus would have said, and Cyrus will remain and be the dragon on guard.'

'I suppose we must start at daylight? It's a great nuisance,' I said, 'having this kind of thing to do over again.'

'You haven't gone mad by any chance,' said the Major, taking a light and peering into my face, 'as the defendant in Racker *v.* Smith did? A ten thousand pound claim *was* something to lose when all the world knew that he was in the right. No, we haven't quite lost No. 4 yet, in spite of the Doctor and all his works. But softening of the brain *must* be setting in, or you would never think of losing an hour, much less a whole night, when there's a rush like this on. No, we've hired a spring-cart and horse by the day, and the fellow will be here with it when the moon rises. You'll have to look slippy.'

'*You* seem in a wonderful state of sanguine anticipation, Major,' I made answer; 'one would think you were totally unfamiliar with the chance of digging life. Doesn't it strike you that our ordinary luck will attend us—all the best claims will be taken up before we get there, or we shall most industriously bottom a duffer, or having by the strangest fluke dropped on to the gutter, it will be proved incontestably that some one has a better right to it? I am sick of the whole thing. I'll stay and shepherd No. 4, and you can take Cyrus and Joe.'

'You be hanged! you're malingering, and I want to shake the blues out of you. You'll be all right in a week. Besides, think of the glorious novelty of the whole affair. We're both ready to hang ourselves here. I don't believe there's a book I haven't read within fifty miles. And I ask you as a brother officer and a gentleman—I mean as a man and a digger, what *are* we to do till that blessed Supreme Court appeal is heard?'

'All right,' I murmured, 'I have no preference, as people in the provinces say about roast fowls at dinner. Who is the Commissioner?'

'Blake himself, no less—ordered off at a moment's notice. They think there's no other man in the service can handle such a crowd as is likely to be camped on the Oxley within three months. Nor is there, by what we hear. He'll have his work cut out for him, too, they say. There are vessels laid on from San Francisco already.'

'It will realise Mick Hord's mild exaggeration of a rush with forty thousand men. I say,

are Merlin and the sergeant and all the rest
coming too ? '

' Everybody but the Clerk of the Bench, they
say.    There's a new one appointed there, a
fellow just out from England.    Goring wrote
me about him ; stammers a bit, but a great
character, they tell me.    A deal of daring origin-
ality about him.    I look forward to him as a kind
of compensation in the circulating library line.'

' Going to keep Joe Bulder ? '

' Not for long ; he must come back and help
Cyrus do nothing, more's the pity ; but we
can't trust the noble Persian's discretion ; and
Joe's head is a very good one, if he'd had any
encouragement early in life to use it instead of
his hands.'

The moon rose, the cart came, and we went.
Nothing was placed in the vehicle but our indis-
pensables in the way of clothes, bedding, our
simple cooking utensils, and of course our tools.
The road lay under our feet in the clear moonlight, white and dusty, between the withered
grass and the tall tree-stems.    The air was
fresh.    The heavens brightly azure.    The horse
was active and powerful, and his owner, well
paid, drove briskly forward.

There was little trouble in finding the road,
which led through the park-like forest which
surrounded Yatala to the plains of the Oxley,
on the head-waters of which this last-found
Eldorado had arisen. Had we felt any un-
certainty it would have been quickly removed,
for in front, behind, on every side were way-
farers journeying to the same goal, of every kind,
in every sort of conveyance, with every description of animal.

Bullock-drays and horse-drays, American
express waggons, hand-carts drawn by men,
and even wheel-barrows propelled by sturdy
arms containing all the household goods of a
family. Women laden with immense bundles
were dragging young children by the hand, or
as often carrying infants at their bosoms.

Sometimes a drove of cattle with wild riders
behind them would come silently and all
ghostly in the moonlight upon the strangely
hurrying crowd ; as silently, too, retreat, only
to move parallel with, but far distant from, the
disturbing concourse, whose physical needs they
were destined to supply.

The whole movement had the appearance of
something between a pilgrimage and a fair

suddenly cut adrift from its moorings, and compelled to travel forward in grotesque procession to another land—so mixed and incongruous did the component parts appear ; so unsuited and unusual to the rude travelling that was imminent, the yet ruder labour to come. I should have enjoyed the humorous contrasts of the scene, but hope deferred had indeed rendered the heart sick—sick unto death, with a despondency as new as oppressive, with a sombre presentiment I tried in vain to shake off.

We travelled day and night, only allowing ourselves needful rest and food, and bearing hard upon the good horse that carried our chattels. On the sixth day we reached the Oxley, and had a free and uninterrupted view of the Great Rush.

It was a strange sight. We, who had seen many goldfields, had never seen one exactly like this before.

The auriferous deposit had been so exceedingly rich in one particular point or cape of land which ran into the river that an unprecedented density of mining settlement had taken place there. This was the famous

'jeweller's shop,' where the very earth seemed
composed of gold dust, with gold gravel for a
variety.    Thousands and tens of thousands of
pounds' worth of the ore had been taken out of
a few square feet here, and no blanks had been
drawn for many yards immediately around.

We were fortunate in meeting a friend we
had known in Ballarat, who immediately gave
us the *carte du pays*.

He himself was such a man as one meets at
goldfields, in the islands of the South Seas, in
the desert, or in London, indifferently and
apparently without any particular reason why
he should be in one place more than another ;
but chiefly in the waste places of the earth,
though he was as much at home in a West-End
drawing-room as here where we found him,
darkly handsome and cool as ever, leaning
against a tall tree trunk, smoking a carefully
coloured meerschaum, and gazing tranquilly
upon the curious human mass below.

'Olivera, as I live ! who in the world would
have thought of seeing you here ? ' said the
Major.

'My dear fellow,' said the stranger, slowly
and impressively, 'this is precisely the place

where you *should* have been certain of finding me. Haven't I been at every Great Rush since California in '49 ? '

'Well, yes, I believe you have ; you're a sort of auriferous wandering Jew. And what does your peripatetic wisdom think of this small assortment of the excellent of the earth ? And hadn't we better join forces ? '

'This will be one of the richest goldfields I have ever set eyes on. My geology and experience are both at fault if it be not so. But I will not join you, for I have been so uniformly unlucky that I believe there is a fate involved in it.'

'Oh, that's all humbug, luck turns ; try again.'

'Mine will turn, but not yet. I shall go on mining to my life's end, for my spirit has never yet yielded to evil fortune ; but no party that I have ever joined has ever been successful, now these many long years, and I will never more share with others my disasters. I dig, as Harry of the Wynd fought, for my own hand. I have a claim, though, worked by wages-men ; and I will point out to you what I think a very favourable conjunction of strata.'

'All right, old man. We bow to your superior wisdom, and place ourselves in your hands—drive on the cart.'

We skirted the great throbbing hive of eager workers spurred up by greed and gain to such desperate efforts that an unnatural silence reigned over the scene. Even their looks were changed. Instead of the frank expression of the ordinary miner, always ready for a little cheerful conversation, these men looked like the worn and troubled artisans of a great factory, where an untimely lassitude or carelessness might lead to the rupture of machinery or the danger of dismissal.

We went down, however, with Olivera to the spot which he pointed out, near which, indeed, his own claim was situated, and under his auspices pegged out four men's ground.

'You see,' he said, 'this is a place where the greenstone and the granite meet. In such a conjunction there is always gold, and heavy gold too.'

'But it was unoccupied before we came. Why did you not take possession of it yourself? You could not know that friends were coming either?'

'My dear boy, if I had taken it up, there would *not* have been gold in it. My luck would have prevented that highly desirable result.'

After pegging out our claim we addressed ourselves to the task of putting up our tent and making ourselves comfortable for the time being.

We had forty-eight hours in which to arrange matters before we were required by law to go to work, so that there was time to spare. We had also to get hold of a fourth man as mate and shareholder, not so easy a matter in a community of strangers.

We wanted a man who could work, also one that would be reasonably easy to live with. A high moral standard we should not insist on; but neither did we care to be troubled with a dissolute rowdy or a drunkard.

The man with the spring-cart had been paid off after depositing our baggage, and was taking a reconnoitring tour preparatory to returning to his family at Yatala.

We had put up our tent, and firmly secured it with pegs and ropes against wind or weather.

We were standing aimlessly watching the un-
ceasing crowd that passed to and fro, like
ghosts in an Inferno, when Joe suddenly uttered
a strongish ejaculation, and relapsed into the
Kentish idiom.

'Danged if I did na think I should see 'un
some day, and it's coomed at last.'

'See who, Joe?' I asked.

'Why, *him*,' quoth my henchman, strongly
excited. 'Dost see yon man a-talking th' chap
in th' red shirt and high boots? That un's
brother Jack, sure enow.'

It had always seemed to us a curious thing
that we should never have met with Mr. Jack
Bulder in the flesh, though his memorable
letter and remittance had been the proximate
cause of our emigration. We had heard of
him repeatedly, sometimes at one place, sometimes at another—in Queensland, Victoria, New
Zealand by turns; but always something had
interfered to prevent his looking up his brother
during all the years that both had been in
Australia.

I turned and saw a good-looking, well-
dressed individual, who did not carry out my
preconceived notion of a forecastle Jack. It

was he, nevertheless.   I watched Joe Bulder
go up to him and say something which caused
him to turn round sharply.   I saw both men
confront and look steadily at each other.   Then
followed a sturdy hand-clasp, which was all
the greeting beyond 'Well, Jack, is't thou, old
man?'—'Why, Joe, I never thought you'ld turn
out half as smart a fellow,'—which was considered necessary by the emigrant Britons after
fifteen years' absence.   They walked over towards me.

'This is my brother Jack, Mr. Pole, him as
wrote the letter as I showed you at Dibblestowe forge,' said Joe with some effort and
shyness.   'You'll remember it.'

'I remember it well enough, Joe,' I said;
'but for it, you and I would never have been
here.   I hope your brother has more to show
for his time than some of us.'

'Glad to see you, sir,' said Mr. Jack Bulder,
raising his hat, and discovering by his address
that the university of travel had sufficed to
impart a polish to which Joe had not attained.
'You're Mr. Pole that my brother came out
with.   It's a good sign he's stuck by you so
long.'

'It has spoken well for both of us,' said I, 'we have been firm friends and true mates all this time. And now, what do you think of this rush?'

'It's the best I've seen yet,' he said promptly. 'And I saw Ballarat at the start. I've been here since the prospector struck gold. I happened to be working in a gully nigh hand when the news came.'

'And how have you done?'

'Well, not so bad. Our party's just broke up, because we worked out the claim. We divided four hundred and fifty a man for three weeks' work.'

'That's good, isn't it?' said Joe; 'worth picking up, eh?'

'Pretty fair,' said the experienced miner, 'but nothing to what some of 'em's doing. I've banked my share, and I'm looking out to nip in again—while the market's up.'

'You can have a share in the claim which we've just pegged out,' said I. 'We want a fourth man, and were, indeed, looking out for one.'

'Whereabouts is it?'

'Close by here—near that greenstone dyke.'

'Oh, if it's there, I'm on. I had some notion of that spot myself; it's as likely a place as anywhere on the field. Now Joe, you and I can wire in and see which is the best man.'

'I'm on,' answered Joe, a ray of humour irradiating his honest countenance. 'I could na work alongside o' thee when thou wast at Dibblestowe. But I reckon I can handle a pick with thee or any other man, now.'

This, of course, was a very fortunate concurrence of events. We had secured a really first-rate worker, and a man of experience on the field. Besides, I took much interest in him, as a brother of Joe's, one of the best and truest fellows that ever broke bread.

The Major, returning after a long talk with Olivera, was pleased to find that we had secured so good a mate. He went through the form of touching the pegs, to ensure strictly legal possession. (A burnt child, etc.) The brothers went away together, presumably to have a good talk, as Englishmen ever do, and unburden their minds.

Soon after daylight next morning they returned, bringing with them on a pack-horse

Jack's tent and worldly possessions, including various mining tools, and other articles more or less useful. This was a convenient arrangement for us, as the brothers agreeing to keep house together, the Major and I had the other tent to ourselves.

Little time was lost in preliminaries. The sun was not high before we had our stage and windlass up, and were delving away at mother earth as if we intended to solve the question of her central fires.

We were none of us new at the trade; there was a certain emulation between the patrician and plebeian element, for we worked in pairs. We were all young and in top condition. The consequence was, we got down at such a pace that more than one of the daily arriving parties stopped, all eager as they were, to wonder at the rapidity with which our beautifully straight and even shaft was boring, as if with a gigantic auger, towards the bed rock.

Olivera used to come and gaze at us, and then go back and inspirit his wages-men with tales of our prowess, they naturally not being quite so anxious to strain every nerve in an enterprise in which they were less directly interested.

Though they had a week's start of us, we bottomed on the same day, and by nightfall the field was aware that Olivera's half-share men had bottomed another duffer, and that Pole and party, from Yatala, were so 'dead on the gutter' that every dish they took out was half gold.

# CHAPTER XIV

IT was certainly one of the richest finds we had any of us encountered, and we had been where the gold lay as plentiful as shells by the seashore. Directly we were down we drove across to the outer edges of our boundary, lest some smart neighbour (for we were closely surrounded by this time) should subterraneously encroach and get into our treasure-chamber before we had full knowledge of its outer walls.

This sort of thing had happened before, within our own knowledge. More than once a too easy party of miners in rich ground had, when down upon the lowest stratum, suddenly found, as they said, 'the bottom drop out of their shaft,' all their hopes of wealth untold falling with it into an unknown abyss.

This abnormal proceeding had resulted from

smarter neighbours having driven, or made
lateral galleries all about their under world,
taking the gold up their own shaft, and perhaps
clearing out altogether to a distance before
their iniquity became manifest.

There was certainly the method of legal
recovery of damages and value of gold so
abstracted, if wilful encroachment and felonious
taking could be fully proved.    But on a
thronged and quickly-shifting alluvial goldfield,
like the Oxley, the chances were against re-
ceiving satisfaction in full.    Probably, too, the
ill-gotten gold was sold or spent before the
discovery was made, transferred almost as far
beyond the bailiff's reach, if a judgment was
obtained, as the quart of whisky which the
Highlander defied the Customs officer to
confiscate.

As I said before, our party was too *rusé* and
experienced to lay itself open to such peculiar
pillage.    We drove and raised our wash-dirt
without anxiety or molestation, and afterwards
separated it from the attendant clay and gravel
by the old-fashioned expedient of a 'tom.'
This abbreviation of 'long tom' is a sufficiently
lengthy trough made of sawn boards with a

plate of perforated iron at one end. The
auriferous gravel, here placed, has a constant
stream of water playing over it, the gold
remaining in crevices specially prepared. Our
wash-dirt was so exceptionally rich that very
little treatment sufficed for it. At the end of
the week's washing up, we discovered that we
were each making at the rate of a thousand
pounds a man, or fifty-two thousand a year. A
most respectable income. Even my friends of
Mid-Kent would have allowed this; though
many of them maintained, to their dying day,
that gold digging was more or less an immoral
occupation.

Well as we were doing, of course many
others in our vicinity and other places were as
richly rewarded. Our claim was soon well known
as the Greenstone Dyke run of gold; one consequence of which was, that every available
yard of soil, for more than a mile round, was
taken up, thus preventing us from extending
our operations, or continuing further search in
the same direction.

We did not mind this, for, in addition to our
present slice of luck, we had, in deference to
Jack Bulder's advice, bought up all the 'in-

terests,' that is, shares, half shares, and quarter
shares on or near the supposed run of gold that
we had struck, which were for sale. We had
cash in hand, and so were able to speculate to
advantage, as many of our neighbours were
poor men, not long come on to the field. So
that when the Greenstone Dyke Lead became
so notoriously lucrative, we had more strings to
our bow than one, and several sources of income.

Yet it seemed very hard that Olivera, who
had shown us the lead and demonstrated by
geological facts that the gold *must* be there,
should get not an ounce of it; his claim being
one of the very few blanks that were recorded
on the lead.

Besides, as all the claim holders had closed
round as far as could be seen in every direction, he was thereby shut out from getting
another claim, even within hail of his first
favourite spot. There was nothing for him but
to go to a distant portion of the field and try
his fortune there. He did so, taking his losses,
as usual, very coolly, only saying 'Just my
luck. There's plenty more on this field, more
than these blockheads dream of, who have

been crowding so eagerly here. But it is rather hard to be almost the only man who has duffered out on *a lead of my own discovering*. But you will do me the justice to say that I expected it from the commencement.'

So Mr. Dycecombe Olivera, whom we had got into the habit of calling The Don, from his dark and somewhat foreign appearance, calmly departed with his vassals, and chose another site for a probable gold mine, about due west of the present workings. This other was due east. Perhaps he thought that a direct antithesis might break the spell.

While we were working together before the successful result of our co-operative enterprise, I had instinctively occupied myself with observing the characteristics of our new mate, Mr. Jack Bulder.

His certainly was an organisation dear to the psychological inquirer. He was much cleverer and more amusing than poor Joe, whom he continually rallied about his simplicity and the close-clinging rusticities he had been unable to shake off.

'Hang it, Joe,' he used to say, 'why, you're just the same yokel as you were when I recollect

you blubbering like a great girl when I went
away to sea.'

'Happen I mightn't see so much to blubber
about, if ye were gannin' noo. When folks
is young they're foolish like. I had na been
long from mother's apron-string then. I'm
none as forrard as thee, I'll allow, but I can do
a many things as I never thout to learn in
foreign parts. And I can work and haud a
still tongue, lad.'

'I never could,' laughed the elder brother.
'I never could in my life ; there you have the
advantage of me, as you will find some day.
However, you *can* work, and no mistake, Joe.
I didn't think there was a man in Yatala, or
here either, who could work alongside of me,
so easy and regular as you have done.'

Jack Bulder did himself no more than justice
when he half stated that no man on the field
could work alongside of him with pick and
shovel in a shaft. He was one of the most
wonderful performers in the shaft-sinking line
that we had ever dropped across. Strong,
quick-witted, and absolutely tireless ; he had
the ready-for-anything turn of mind of a trained
sailor. Full, also, of mechanical expedients in

any emergency, he displayed a fertility of re-
source which furnished the most unaffected
astonishment to his brother. Joe could not
sufficiently express his wonderment at such a
genius having appeared from out of the Bulder
family, and their surroundings in Mid-Kent.

' Danged if I know whether it be the sailor-
ing or the digging as has made thee the man
thou art,' said he, in one of his vain attempts
to explain the transformation which had taken
place in his elder. ' Seems to me as if they
sent all the young chaps frae Dibblestowe
aboord ship for five year, and to the diggin' for
five year more, they'd never want no poor law
nor unions. Why, half-a-dozen chaps like
Jack 'd make the fortune o' a dozen towns like
Dibblestowe ; they'd toorn all the ploughmen
into farmers, and all the farmers into squires—
danged if they wouldn't.'

Without going quite so far as our worthy
Joe in his theories as to the best means of vital-
ising the latent forces of the peasantry of Britain,
the Major and I did full justice to the merits of
our new comrade. We had always regarded
Joe as the model Englishman of the labouring
class ; but his senior had all his unerring com-

mon sense, propriety of feeling, and incalculable staying power, apparently, with far more initiative faculty.

Whether it was the seafaring or the digging experience which had made the man he was of him, we, of course, could not determine. Anyhow, he was an interesting psychological study, and as such, afforded endless matter for reflection and comparison to the Major and myself.

Not that we, after our dearly bought and curiously varied experience, were too prone to take the most attractive new acquaintance wholly upon trust. Hundreds of human disappointments, personal and vicarious, had served to cure us of the Arcadian trustfulness with which we might have entered Australia. Indeed, the half - reproachful conclusion was strictly applicable to us, which passed sadly from the lips of a *détenu* in the cells of one of Her Majesty's metropolitan gaols.

Two prisoners in the exercise yard, serving their sentence, were heard one day conversing in earnest tones, such as aroused the attention of the warder, watchful lest plots for breaking gaol should be incubating. It proved merely to be the discussion of the probable success of

an appeal to the Head of the Department—
formerly a Commissioner of Goldfields—for
some alleviation of duress.

'Do yer think we could gammon the chief
bloke, Bill?' said the milder ruffian. 'He
looked a good-'arted cove when we see him
last?'

'I'm afeard it's no go,' croaked Bill, with
despairing cadence, 'he's been too long at them
bloomin' diggins.'

Such, alas! had been our too realistic destiny.
Without losing our reverence for the higher
qualities of our common nature, we had learned
to distinguish between the true and the false;
and, for most purposes of deceit and imposture,
such as are unblushingly practised upon the
excellent of the earth—we had been 'too long
at the diggings!'

'Confound the fellow,' said the Major one
day, when we had had a lengthened discussion
about him; 'he's as good as a new novel, very
nearly. But for him, and a torn copy of *Adam
Bede*, I should have been out of all intellectual
rations—perhaps taken to beer and dominoes.
Still [reflectively], he's got one fault, a very
bad one, in my experience of character, real

and fictitious. I can't call to mind a faultless hero, who hadn't a screw loose somewhere, connected with the leading machinery, too. Now, our friend's too d—d perfect altogether. I'm sorry for it. But mark my words, Pole, there's something *to find out about him.*'

We, therefore, placed a percentage of our judgment, while basking in the sunshine, to the suspense account, so to speak, of Mr. Jack Bulder's energy and capacity; for, did he not splice our rope, much worn and not to be replaced, improvise an anvil and point out picks after hours, manufacture a superior kind of windlass with a patent brake, and twice the ordinary power, besides fishing out a new auriferous gully, before Olivera, who, however, endorsed his judgment and took up a claim broadside on to us? This, of course, was after we had worked out our 'goldsmith's window,' as the adjacent diggers christened it, and recommenced to dig out another fortune.

Our first claim possessed the very great advantage of being easy to work, besides being fabulously rich; that is, the wash-dirt could be got out and treated with almost a tithe of the terrible work and loss of time necessary at poor old Yatala. So Jack and his brother working all the time like two benevolent Trolls, with zealous emulation, it came to pass that we were clean worked out and had sold the good-will of our claim to some new arrivals for 'a cool hundred,' before many of our neighbours at Greenstone Gully were half done with their 'dirt.'

As may be easily imagined, this assimilation of the 'root of all evil' to the familiar tuber which merely needs in ordinary seasons to be dug up and put in bags (ours were chamois leather, to be sure), was not without its effect upon society at large, civilised and uncivilised.

Rumour had caught up, magnified, and sent fleeing on the wings of the wind to every quarter of the globe, sensational inflations, gold-coloured and rose-hued, until all Europe, Africa, America, and even Asia, to the bounds of 'far Cathay,' grew familiar with the gold farms on the banks of the Oxley, where the crops were gathered all the year round; where the streams trickled over treasure untold, and the very rocks were of virgin gold!

Our own astonishing successes, and, indeed, those of numberless fellow-workers, could not fail to produce a violent commotion among the floating populations of the earth. But Aladdin-chamber inventories must have been sown broadcast to account for the tidal-wave of stranger hosts which now came rolling in upon the river flats of the Oxley.

Not only did every colony of Australia, every province of New Zealand, send in, apparently, its able-bodied contingent, but Americans, Canadians, Germans, Frenchmen, Italians, Swiss, Cockneys and Highlanders, Scots and Irishmen, Spaniards and West-Indian Creoles, arrived, apparently in shiploads.

Moreover, and on this modern invasion our conscript fathers looked darkly and with sullen disapproval, long strings of Chinese, grotesquely attired, and heavily burdened, came thronging along the well-worn trail which led from the arterial highways of the coast.

Simultaneously with the advance in force of the great army of miners, an official camp had been formed, where Captain Blake took up his headquarters, accompanied by Mr. Merlin, the sergeant, and a strong body of police, further reinforced a few days afterwards.

The Commissioner, with military prevision,

selected as a site a high bluff or point surrounded on three sides by the deep and rapid waters of the Oxley. A stout palisaded fence was at once run across the neck (a narrow one) on the side facing the diggings, thus forming a convenient paddock for the troop horses, while, as a strategical position, it was capable of scientific defence, should the need ever arise.

The tents were pitched, pending the erection of the necessary buildings, the horses let loose, the Captain's dogs chained up, the Union Jack flaunted on a sapling appropriate for a flagstaff, and Her Majesty's Government was fully represented.

It was apparent to us that it would take the Commissioner and Mr. Merlin 'all their time,' as the diggers phrased it, to keep the field in the same state of order and subjection as had obtained at Yatala. A better *sous-officier* than Sergeant M'Mahon they could not possibly have had. But, beside the enormously increased population which now gave every sign of being massed upon the ground, there were other elements likely to be infused which might lead to revolt and disorganisation.

On the first Saturday afternoon, after having

heard that the new Clerk of the Bench had arrived, we went to call upon him.   He was also Mining Registrar, Agent for the Curator of Intestate Estates, Registrar of the Small-Debts Court, Coroner, Commissioner for Affidavits, and the holder of several other minor offices, which are generally appendages to the appointment.

We found him in the large tent which did duty as a court-house, of one corner of which he had possessed himself.   Evidently not a man of method, he was surrounded with books and papers relating to his office, all in such a state of inextricable confusion, that an average licensed surveyor (of all men, perhaps, most experienced in making a tent habitable and officially effective) would have swooned on the spot.

' Now then, w-w-what's your name,' he called out in a loud voice, without looking up, 'don't keep me w-w-waiting all d-d-day.'

The Major smiled.   He looked up angrily. ' How d-d-dare you presume to l-l-laugh, sir, in Her M-m-majesty's t-t-tent, sir, taking up the G-g-government time ?   D-d-don't you know every minute of my t-t-time's worth a g-g-guinea ? '

The Major having by this time extracted his
card, presented it, at the same time saying,
' Mr. Bagstock, I believe, permit me to intro-
duce my friend Mr. Pole.'

Mr. Bagstock gave one hurried glance at
the card, stared wildly at us, then with a rapid
alteration of manner, got up and shook hands
warmly with us.

' D-d-delighted to see you, I'm sure.  Charlie
Grant—b-b-best f-f-fellow in the world—
s-s-said you were out here.  W-w-wrote, I
believe.   Live near this p-p-pandemonium ? '

' We live *in* it,' said the Major; ' we're
familiar demons.'

' But wh-wh-what do you d-d-do, then ? '

' Dig,' I said, ' and are not badly paid for it
just at present.'

' Regular miners ? ' said our new acquaintance, still wonderingly.  ' Good God! you don't
say so.  Got one of th-these and all ? '  Here
he pointed to a book of Miners' Rights, upon
which he had been scribbling names as fast
as he could write before we came in, which
accounted for his unconventional reception.

This he explained as we talked afterwards,
during which conversation he showed himself

a most amusing man of the world. His habit
of stammering was so repeatedly useful in
giving point and accentuation to his witticisms,
that we doubted seriously as to whether it was
natural or assumed.

A vein of eccentricity, amounting to recklessness, pervaded his character, which I thought
could either be accepted by the mining population as legitimate humour and pleasantry, or be
seriously disapproved of, and so lead to the
severance of official relations.

He freely confided to us his views as to
the performance of his duties, as well as his
general opinion as to the best mode of treating
the heterogeneous population with which he
was brought into contact.

' F-f-firmness, my dear fellow, and k-k-keep-
ing them in their p-p-places ; depend upon it,
that's the l-l-line to take, and cut s-s-short all
their d—d t-t-technical details.'

' Hulloo ! what is it ?  Ex-c-c-cuse me,
M-m-major ? '

Here a burly digger advanced with a document carefully folded up in his hands.

' Are you the gen'l'man as takes the haffer-
davys ? '

'C-c-certainly; all I can g-g-get.'

'Well, Mr. Cramp said as I was to make my hafferdavy afore you, where you see my mark here, as I was the owner of these town allotments in Bathurst.'

'All r-r-right, s-s-swear away.'

Here he looked around for the official Bible, which ought to have been within reach, but which was probably buried under some of the piles of papers, books, forms of summons, warrants, informations, etc., which lay around as if in upheaval a corner of a stationer's shop had fallen in just then.

Not seeing it he continued: 'This is your signature, and the contents of this affidavit are t-t-true, so h-h-help you God. Half a guinea!'

The man looked rather confused and uncertain, but produced the coin, and then said, 'I didn't see no Bible, sir?'

'N-n-never mind. K-k-kiss the book when you g-g-get home!'

Overawed by the authority and impressiveness of Mr. Bagstock's manner, the miner, not one of the pestilent educated sort, departed, and we only awaited his safe clearing out to laugh heartily.

'Allow me to congratulate you upon your *savoir faire*,' said the Major with much politeness. 'For a newly-landed official, I don't recollect seeing your equal.'

Bagstock confronted us with a face of absolute gravity.

'Where do you s-s-suppose I should be if I d-d-didn't cut short these f-f-fellows' trifling objections? C-c-can't waste the G-g-government time, you know.'

There was a humorous twinkle in his eye as he said this, which nearly set us off again; but his command of feature was perfect. So, arranging for him to dine with us and Olivera on the following day, and promising to send a guide to the camp before the appointed hour, we took our leave.

'By Jove,' said the Major, 'our friend will either be a distinguished ornament to the service, or he will be mentioned in such a way in Blake's despatches that the Government will require his services at Bourke or Wilcannia without delay.'

'I don't know about that,' I said. 'He has plenty of "pluck and assurance," as Deuchatel said the other day, and foreseeing rather wild times, I incline to the belief that he will develop into a celebrity.'

'Talking of distinguished people,' said my companion, 'I heard one of these Victorians, who are arriving in such hordes, address Jack Bulder familiarly by a different name. The man evidently knew him well. He acknowledged him, but little more, and went on with his work. He looked up afterwards and said something about "a purser's name being handy now and then in this country."'

'What did the fellow call him ?'

'Dawson, I think ; not his own name, at any rate.'

'It can't matter to us,' I said ; 'he may have married, and since he was on the diggings, as the men say, and have reasons not affecting his general character for not wishing to be brought back under a warrant, to answer a charge of maintenance. Such things happen now and then. Look at Westerman's case.'

'I am surprised to hear a man of your high moral tone talk in that way,' said the Major sarcastically. 'No, I don't think our accomplished friend, somehow, fears that the flowery fetters of matrimony may resolve themselves into prosaic handcuffs; but I am convinced he has reason to dread some *éclaircissement* or other.   In spite of his ceaseless work—and he is the devil, *bon diable* if you will, at that— he has a restless look.   And I wouldn't give *very* heavy odds that he doesn't drink.'

'Why, he never touches anything,' said I, greatly astonished.

'Bad sign,' replied the Major, 'very bad; that is the reason why I think so.'

Our speculations were, however, confined to our own breasts.   In the daily increasing rout and turmoil of the greatest concourse of people ever gathered together upon (temporarily) the richest goldfield in Australia, it did not appear to matter much about private character, more than upon the moral standard reached by any given soldier in a decisive battle.

Our time was much taken with our own highly exciting work, for which we were still rewarded beyond our most sanguine expectations.   As all the early comers were similarly successful, and as it was from time to time requisite to defend one's ground against aggressive strangers, ignorant of mining or, apparently, any other laws, there was absolutely

no leisure whatever. The Commissioner rode
his horses almost to death, having to decide
so many hundreds of cases on the ground
daily; and though rapid and decisive as usual,
the immense population of the field, with its
daily multiplying gold areas, employed every
moment of daylight, and still left a margin of
small disputes undisposed of.

It was in one of these where our new mate
distinguished himself by prompt action peculiar
to himself. One afternoon we discovered that
four unprepossessing-looking strangers had
pegged out a corner of our claim, and were
proceeding to sink thereon, under the pretext
that we held more than our proper quantity,
and that there was 'spare ground between us
and the next claim.' It was merely a pretext,
as we knew, but annoying, as it might be a
week or two now before the Commissioner
could come down and adjudicate. Before
which time, as the ground was shallow, these
fellows might have their shaft down and com-
mence to rob us in daylight.

It must be explained that so rich was the
yield of gold at this particular gully, every foot
of ground represented no inconsiderable sum.

A certain number of superficial feet only was allotted to each miner by the regulations. If he, working separately, or his party collectively, occupied more than the legal allowance, any other miner, making the discovery, might take possession of it, as ground held in excess, and if he proved his case it was allotted to him by the Commissioner.

Hence, in rich localities, it was customary for men to go round the claims with a tape-line carefully measuring the areas. If they discovered a sufficient quantity of ground 'held in excess,' barely sufficient to sink a shaft upon, they made a practice of taking possession of it. In some cases they managed to work these fragments of claims, and secure a portion of the general treasure ; in others they effected a compromise, and sold out their titles to the original holders. This was not held to be a manly or reputable course of conduct by the miners generally, and, indeed, was chiefly adopted by the loafers and scamps of the goldfield. But, on the other hand, no miner had any right to take up more ground than he was legally entitled to, and if he was thereby damaged it was his own fault.

We, however, and also Olivera, had always been scrupulously careful to measure accurately our due and lawful quantity, holding it for the reasons recited wrong and inexpedient to do otherwise. We were, therefore, convinced that the attempted occupation was only an impudent struggle for blackmail, by forcibly encroaching on our claim.

The Major and I had resisted by all means, short of personal violence, this invasion of our rights, and were engaged in a stormy altercation with the leading man of the party, a tall, fair-bearded, dissipated-looking personage. He affected an American accent, but was evidently one of those pernicious scoundrels, known as 'whitewashed Yankees,' who, having been a few years in the States, make the fact an excuse for imitating the alleged license of the worst class of American rowdies.

'Now, look here, mister,' he was saying when the two brothers came up, 'ye don't allow, I guess, that we've come all the way from Bear Valley to let you Britishers freeze on to every likely gulch you con-clude to mark out on this all-fired rich placer. No, sirree. I reckon there's a smart chance of one handy now, and hyar goes my peg.'

Suiting the action to the word, he raised a stout pointed sapling end and prepared to drive it into the earth. At the same moment Jack Bulder with his brother Joe appeared on the scene, having both stripped to their working clothes for the shift.

Walking rapidly up, the elder brother appeared to have fully comprehended the situation, and backed up sturdily by Joe, was evidently ready to carry out mine or the Major's order. In the moment he cast eyes upon the tall man his manner changed suddenly and remarkably.

He rushed forward and, for a moment, his eyes glared at the stranger with an expression of hate, loathing, and wrath unspeakable, almost demoniac in intensity, which distorted his whole countenance. The direst earthly tragedy could furnish no fitter exposition.

His enemy—for such he was, doubtless, and the feud was not of yesterday—gazed at him with an air of deepest surprise, mingled with dismay.

'So it's you? blast you!' he hissed out,

'thief and betrayer that you are; hasn't the earth swallowed you up yet? Drop your peg and clear while you can. Why should I have your blood on my head? curse you! You won't?—then——'

Wholly dominated, as it seemed, by uncontrollable, furious passion, and, indeed, hardly giving his antagonist time to do anything, who stood speechless, still holding the peg, John Bulder dashed in upon him with the agility of a panther, and with scarcely less ferocity.

Pushing aside with his right hand the stake held cudgel-fashion as if it had been a walking-cane, he struck the stranger such a blow with his left as only an Englishman, early trained by the village *lanista*, can inflict. Down went the man prone, without sense or motion, and his antagonist stood beside him for one moment grinding his teeth and looking at the bleeding face, as one who hesitated whether he should follow up his natural instincts and stamp the life out of his foe as he lay beneath his feet.

At the same instant Joe Bulder walked forward and in a sort of mechanical manner knocked down the man nearest to him. All conflict being highly contagious, the Major and

I advanced, upon which the others of the invading party threw up their hands with a gesture of disavowal, and declined the combat, temporarily.

'You seem rather hot property, mates,' said the more respectable-looking one of the twain. 'I'm not agin a friendly round, when everything's agreeable ; but it strikes me there's been enough rough and tumble for one morning. Yankee Jake brought us here ; he said he knowed the ropes, and it was the regular thing to go in and jump a bit of ground or we'd never get none.'

'Well, now that you've discovered that it's a highly irregular thing,' said the Major, 'perhaps you'd oblige me by clearing out, and taking Mr. Yankee Jake with you, alive or dead.   He looks like the last.'

That distinguished individual not being quite dead, slowly raised himself and looked around with an air of deadliest malice at his foe, who stood near him, as if with wrath unsated.

'Get up,' he said, 'you hound, and take your rotten carcass out of my sight.   Why don't I drive my knife into you and make an end of it ?   It's almost worth while.'

Jack looked so tigerish, as he glanced at the bleeding wretch, laying his hand upon the sheath-knife which, sailor fashion, he always wore at his belt, that the man hastily, though with difficulty, arose, and, assisted by his mates, limped off the claim towards the place where their bundles lay. Before finally departing the tall man turned towards us, and with a face hardly human in its expression, bleeding and distorted as it was, groaned out—

' I owe you another for this, Ballarat Jack— d'ye hear? and I'll pay it yet, as sure as my name's Jake Challerson.'

The man whom he addressed made no answer, but with his hat over his eyes, and his breast still heaving with suppressed passion, passed into his tent. The only practical answer to the menace was that of Joe Bulder, who, tearing up their pegs, flung them after the retreating party.

There was no ulterior consequence to this rather serious affray, such as would on the morrow, as surely as it dawned, have taken place at Yatala. But the enemy, for reasons of their own probably, did not invoke the aid of the civil power. The police had their hands

full of criminal cases and matters of more
pressing import. And the Commissioner,
when he heard of it, said he wished to heaven
that other miners would take example by
Pole and party, and not bother him about every
trumpery jumping dispute.

We were not sorry to be done with our
dispute on such easy terms, having had enough
of law to last us our lives. Jack appeared to
have done the right thing at the right time, as
usual ; still we could not help being impressed
by the exaggerated ferocity which he had ex-
hibited in his encounter with the tall stranger.

'Those men were old miners, that was plain
enough,' said the Major, 'and foes of no
ordinary degree. I never saw mortal look
more like a demon than Jack Bulder did after
he had knocked the fellow down : and he did
drop him, like a bullock. Never saw a
straighter blow, fair in the mouth too. He
won't eat or talk "worth a cent," as he would
say himself, for some time to come.'

'And that ruffian hates him with no ordinary
hatred either,' I said. 'I wonder what it is all
about ?'

'*Must* have been a woman mixed up with

it,' mused the Major, with grim certainty; 'no real hell-broth without *her* finger in it, trust me.'

'Pooh, pooh, Major, you're too hard upon the sex, altogether. Diggers quarrel about scores of things, apart from any question of that sort, as we know.'

'Quarrel, perhaps. But there is that kind of feud between those two men, if I mistake not, that only blood will quench, if opportunity serves. What did that scoundrel mean by calling him Ballarat Jack, too? Anything to do with the stockade affair?'

'Shouldn't wonder; but there were lots in it as well if he *was* there. He doesn't talk much about his Victorian experiences, I notice. By the way, how's Olivera?'

'Well, I believe he's done rather better than usual for him. His party got £500 out of their last claim, which will about pay wages and something over. This is the fifth claim he has been in since he came here, and the first in which he has seen the colour. Isn't it wonderful? But I have known cases like it,' continued the Major, 'though rarely where the seeker was so persevering and scientific as our friend here.    However, if the gold holds out, his luck *must* turn some day.    No one ever knew the red to turn up for more than a certain number of times.'

'I suppose he'll be all right if the gold holds out, but a few years at this rate will see it out.'

'*He* says another generation won't, nor another after that,' replied the Major, 'that it's mathematically demonstrable.'

# CHAPTER XV

WHILE these minor events had been but ruffling the tide of time—ah me! what mere ripples upon the shoreless sea are all our lives, our deaths, all fateful agony between!—the great gold-seeking multitude had swelled by constant influx to the population of a province.

There was no hill or dale within miles of the Commissioner's tents but was covered with tents and huts. The forest was crowded with grazing horses and working oxen. At night the vast illuminated area resembled an army encamped, an illusion to which the not infrequent rattle, as of musketry, as the miners discharged their firearms and loaded afresh, lent a reality.

When, in addition to the legitimate mining population, it was known that by far the greater number of the bad characters and escaped

criminals from all the colonies had flocked
hither in aid of whatever contingent might
arrive from foreign sources, it may be guessed
what a task lay before the officials in maintain-
ing order and good government.

Certainly, trifling reinforcements had arrived,
in the shape of more police, as also a couple of
sub-commissioners, who, under Captain Blake's
guidance, adjudicated in the less important
cases which now arose in endless succession.

An escort, duly organised, left the camp
weekly, with such an amount of gold stowed
away in iron-bound boxes as would have gone
far to induce the buccaneers in old Morgan's
day to have landed at Sydney and marched
across the continent for the express purpose of
securing it.  All things were apparently working fairly well in groove and gear, yet were
there not wanting signs that awoke doubt in
the minds of those who, like us, had for long
years 'followed the diggings.'

'Strangers and pilgrims,' of all kinds and
castes, were now so common that we should
not have been a whit surprised to see the Cham
of Tartary or the Sandjiack of Bosnia, each
attended by a select body-guard in chain-mail,

ride down Regent Street, as our main arterial thoroughfare, miles long, and crowded on every foot of frontage with shops and dwellings, was designated. Nothing was more common than to see tourists, whose every expression of speech and apparel showed their total want of connection with the community, appear and disappear after a short sojourn with magic suddenness.

One Sunday morning, resting from our labours, the Major and I were at the camp, enjoying the rare luxury of a little *causerie* with the Commissioner and his subalterns, when we remarked four horsemen passing the outer edge of the palisades towards a track which led adown and across a ford in the river.

Not ordinary bushmen, they were sufficiently near the type to be recognised as Australians by people of our experience. Their lounging seat upon their horses, yet with a certain air of litheness and instinctive ease not so observable in riders of European birth, settled the question in our minds. More than one wore the loose cloak or wrap of stout woollen cloth, now commencing to be in common use, borrowed from the wild horsemen of the Pampas, and

hence known as 'ponchos.' Another peculiarity
which did not escape our notice was the
unusually high quality of the horses they
rode.

'Come here, sergeant,' said the Captain,
motioning to that veteran, who at a short
distance was intently observing the *cortège*,
'did you ever see any of those fellows before ?
I don't like the look of them. Depend upon it,
they are after no good.'

The sergeant saluted with due precision, and,
standing very erect, thus delivered himself—

'Well known to the police, Captain, every
mother's son of them! The man on the black
horse is Frank Lardner  The big man next
him is Ben Wall, one's a Victorian native, the
other hails not far from Yedden Mountain ;
both have been up for cattle and horse stealing, "done time," too. I don't see O'Rourke.
There's Gilbert Hawke and young Daly—
dangerous characters, the whole lot.'

' And can't you d-d-do anything t-t-to them ?'
said Mr. Bagstock. 'L-l-lock 'em up or anything as a c-c-caution ; *pour encourager l-l-l-les
autres*, you know.'

' No charge against any of them at present,

eh, sergeant ? ' said the Commissioner.   ' No
warrant ? '

'Not so much as a summons, Captain, or
sureties for the peace—or it would be a grand
chance entirely to take the lot.   I know where
they're going to-night ; and I'm as sure as we
stand here that there's some villainy in the
wind, if we could only get to hear of it in
time.'

' P-p-prevention's better than c-c-cure,' said
Mr. Bagstock oracularly.   ' I should l-l-lay them
by the h-h-heels now, before they've d-d-done
anything.'

' Must act legally, my dear fellow,' said the
Commissioner, smiling ; 'we can't go beyond a
reasonable amount of benevolent despotism in a
British colony.   The law must be respected,
and the liberty of the subject.'

'What's the g-g-good of their being
s-s-subjects, if you c-c-can't take away their
liberty?' argued the advocate, somewhat before
his age, of the yet undeveloped Jingoism.
'L-l-lock 'em up n-n-now, Commissioner, all
for their g-g-good.'

As we thus discussed their characters and
prospects, a turn of the road brought the free

companions in front of where we were standing.
One and all looked steadily at our group; the
leading horseman, indeed, touching his hat in
a natural and unstudied way as they rode by.
I could not but admire, after a fashion, the well-
knit muscular figures, the keen, alert, hunter-
like appearance of these probable bandits.
The careless *abandon* of their horsemanship
gave them a kind of picturesque air not wholly
devoid of romance, and I wished them from my
heart a better fate.

'*Morituri te salutant*, O Proconsul!' murmured the Major. 'I suppose all these fellows
will be shot or hanged within the next year or
two.'

'Very highly probable, indeed,' answered
Blake. 'And before that desirable event takes
place it will have cost the lives of better men.
It is a thousand pities I can't take Bagstock's
advice. In some countries that I have been in
there would have been a way of managing a
*lettre de cachet* for such known desperadoes.'

'I suppose trial by jury and all that kind of
thing agrees best with the British constitution
in the long-run,' said the Major, 'but depend
upon it there's nothing like martial law at a

pinch. The time may come when we shall be glad to resort to it here.'

'Things are not so bad as all that,' said the Commissioner. 'Rather a serious row between the Donegals and the Cornishmen on the South Lead last Sunday night. I hear two of them and one of the Cousin Jacks were nearly killed outright. We shouldn't have allowed that at Yatala. But here we have a surplus population. Perhaps they'll reduce it in their own way.'

'Things are not going on as well as Blake thinks,' said the Major, as we strolled homeward. 'He has had great luck in holding down difficult populations, I grant. But his bridge may break with him some day, and it is as likely to be here as anywhere.'

'That other inspector of police that came over to stay a week or so last month, said he believed all the "cross boys" of all the colonies were congregated here; that there was bound to be a row—by which he meant a revolt, I suppose—and that nothing, in his opinion, could prevent it.'

'They can't hurt us if we're not slain outright, like Sir Albany Fetherstonhaugh in the old border ballad by hard-riding Dick Clym o' the Cleugh, and the rest. Our gold is pretty regularly transmitted by escort. They won't rob that, I suppose.'

'Why not?' I said. 'You don't suppose they have any particular delicacy about stopping that or any other drag with treasure aboard! Fellows like those we saw to-day would be an ugly lot to meet in one of those narrow rocky gaps, as they call them, over the line of ranges.'

'Not pluck enough,' said the Major. 'Horse-stealing and cattle-lifting are their favourite pastime, but standing before a police rifle, or a brace of revolvers held moderately straight, is not in the line of the native-born Australian brigand.'

'I hope you are a true prophet; but I hold a different opinion. These fellows, all unused to warfare as of course they are, are never averse to stand a shot or two for value received. But, like all Australians, when tempted to work or fight, they believe that the risk should not be disproportioned to the gain.'

'All the vices must be here by this time,' mused the Major. 'Even a modest assortment of the virtues is about to join us—from Warraluen, they say, even. The reefers, though on good gold there they say, are so worked on by the marvellous tales of the South Lead here, that they are nearly all leaving in a body, headed by your friend Black Ned. Have you seen Malgrade yet?'

'No, I heard of him though. He hasn't been here long. He camps down at that flat where those fellows we saw near the camp were making for. He and Poynter are working together, they say, and that big fellow with the whiskers, Harry Jefferson. He keeps the Pick and Pan public-house, and it's a rendezvous for all the horse thieves, homicides, and mixed ruffians on this side of the country. Blake told Merlin he ought to make a raid there some day; that it was a regular Alsatia.'

'There's something in the air, I'm convinced. We shall hear news before long. There's a lot of these foreign fellows about that were at the Ballarat stockade. Joe Bulder says, too, there's a good deal of grumbling about the Chinamen.'

'It seems they have been mopping up some rich surfacing, and rather anticipated the European miners, who didn't like it.'

'Didn't they, indeed!' said the Major sardonically. 'Well I must say that for a nice, peaceful appointment, involving no special anxiety, or vexed questions of law or equity, commend me to the post of Commissioner on a large, newly broken-out goldfield.'

'I agree with you most thoroughly,' I replied. 'Taking the character of the population, the ceaseless complaints and disputes, the accidents and offences, the utter impossibility of foreseeing in what consequences the smallest ground of dissatisfaction if left unsettled may result, the complicated criminal and social ramifications underlying the whole fabric, on my honour, if I had a favourite enemy and could ensure his doing his work conscientiously, I would beseech

"The Fiend, to whom belongs
The vengeance due to all our wrongs,"

to present him with the appointment.'

It seems unnecessary to state that nearly all our Yatala friends and acquaintances, as well as numberless strangers, were now located here.

Some of the streets were so full of well-known names and faces that it appeared as if a portion of our old gold town had been lifted up bodily by a genie, as in the *Arabian Nights*, and dropped softly down upon the banks of the Oxley.

In all the earlier gold settlements, only those who had very good interests to represent stayed behind. As for Cyrus, he used to send disconsolate and wonderfully spelled letters, bewailing his lot at having to remain at a place where he could neither work nor play, where he had nothing to do but watch a shaft, and where there was now no more chance of a horse race than there was of a circus in a tea-tree scrub. He had a good mind, he said, to chuck up the whole thing and make tracks for the Oxley.

Not only friends but foes had naturally been borne in on the resistless wave of the exodus. Malgrade and Isaac Poynter, having joined unto them divers other evil spirits worse than themselves, were pursuing their old courses, from the circumstances of the place, with more unchecked license than of old. They had located themselves at a rich and strictly disorderly section of the goldfield, which had early gained an unenviable notoriety. More than one violent death had occurred there. Missing men, known to have left for town with gold, had never again been seen alive. A wild humorist had complimented it with the suggestive title of 'Murderers' Flat.' And, somehow, it had not lost

the ominous name.  Here were congregated,
confessedly, the more lawless spirits of the
place.  Hither came outlaws from other
colonies, over whose heads were warrants of
apprehension certain to be executed if once
their identity were established.  This was the
cover drawn by the police when any criminal of
distinction was wanted ; and on such occasions
Mr. Merlin and his troopers invariably looked
carefully to their arms, and neglected no precaution which might be necessary against surprise or resistance.

'From information received,' the sergeant
was enabled to inform his superior officer that
here the four mounted men who had passed the
camp in the evening had remained during all
the preceding day and night ; that they had
stabled their horses at the hostelry of Mr.
Henry Jefferson, the Pick and Pan, where Malgrade had been seen in their company, besides
other marked men ; that in his, the informant's
opinion, 'something good had been put up,' the
nature of which benevolent enterprise he had
not as yet been enabled to discover.

'So far, so bad,' Mr. Merlin condescended
to remark.  'It would have been something to

the purpose if you had got the least inkling of
*what* they were going to have a shy at. I could
have told *him* that Lardner, Wall, and Gilbert
Hawke had something on hand. What it is
we're all in the dark about. What if we arrest
the lot on suspicion of horse-stealing. I'll swear
they never came honestly by their mounts.'

'Better wait,' counselled the sergeant.
They're bound to be at some new game before
long.'

'How do you know you'll have them then?'
demanded Mr. Merlin fiercely. 'What with
the confounded Donegal riots, and these infernal
Chinamen, coming over here like locusts; and
the cursed dance-houses; and just half the
police here we ought to have—the superinten-
dent keeps one so devilish short of men—the
field is going to the devil; and I expect everything and everybody will come to grief.'

Really, there did seem to be some ground for
Mr. Merlin's slightly bilious deliverance. His
order-loving soul was daily vexed by reason of
the irregularities which he was obliged to
condone, knowing full well, too, that apparent
trifles were prone to swell to dangerous dimen-
sions.

Yet he relaxed not one jot or tittle of daily
or nightly diligence ; every one under his command was kept at the utmost tension of discipline possible to mortal man.

We, in a general way, thought that the
greater concourse of adventurers massed together from so many different sources might,
under unfavourable conditions, drift towards
disaffection and revolt.   But gold, the universal
lubricator, was available in any quantity in
those flush times, and to its efficacy we and all
the moderates were fain to trust.

Truth to tell, we did not trouble ourselves
deeply concerning the social life of the goldfields, or those difficulties which might beset a
conscientious police-officer in the discharge of
his duties.   We were sufficiently heedless of
the morrow to disregard the future of the portion of Australia in which we found ourselves.
We felt a benign trust in those who might
come after.   As long as we were not robbed
or murdered—contingencies against which we
felt tolerably certain of defence—we left all
other considerations to fate and the lesser
providences.

Then our daily labour was engrossing, its

compensation profuse and exciting. If we could only manage to hold on, filling our pails at the golden spring which welled up so plentifully, all Australia might revert to a state of pliocene plasticity for anything we cared.

# CHAPTER XVI

IT is strange to note—stranger still to attempt to reason out the cause why, with such apparent unfairness, the gifts of fortune are in this world bestowed. Nowhere is the anomaly more glaring than on a goldfield. The widest divergence there apparently obtains between the abstractly just and the actual disposition of the prizes so long concealed by jealous Nature. The abstemious cultured toiler, careful for an absent wife and poorly-provided family, is steeped in endless ill-luck ; while the bacchanal, the spendthrift, ay, the felon shedder of innocent blood, drives his pick into the golden heap at will. Who can reconcile these contradictions of circumstance with the eternal verities ?

Thus, in despite of all moral obligations, and with but little apparent regard for the doctrine of compensation, the claims immediately around

Murderers' Flat, unenviable locale as it might
seem, yielded marvellously. Excepting the
original 'Jewellers' Point,' there was no richer
spot on the whole field. The prize-fighters
and 'forcats,' burglars and bushrangers, who
were said to be in a majority thereabouts,
secured lawful gains of such value in a few
weeks as should have converted them to virtuous ways their whole lives after.

So it might well have been. But the chief
result of the wondrous gold spring, here so
easily tapped, was a saturnalia comprehending a
succession of terrible orgies, such as even in the
darkest prison days the land had never known.

Here, fallen to the level of the dregs of
humanity, could Algernon Malgrade reside,
careless of all things but of the huge gains
which he was apparently heaping up; while
associating and carousing in his hours of abandonment with the vilest offscourings of society.
Here was Dolores to be seen flaunting in
extravagant silks and loaded with jewellery.
And here, urged on by the same fatal thirst for
gold, did Edward Morsley propose to settle
afresh, bringing with him his wretched despairing wife.

Of this fresh shuffling of the cards in the game of gold, amid the stakes of which my own life seemed so strangely commingled, I was first informed by common rumour ; more accurately soon after by a letter from poor Jane herself. The miserable, tear-stained missive ran—

'How can I find words to tell you that my husband has determined to leave here for the Oxley, and, worse than all a thousand times, to keep an inn at that horrible place, Murderers' Flat, of which I have heard such dreadful tales. He says we can make a fortune in a year. But I know the sort of life I shall lead there, the insults I shall be exposed to, the daily degradation in which I shall be compelled to share. I feel more than ever inclined to put an end to myself before this last horror comes upon me. I have borne enough, too much, and I solemnly swear that I will not consent to live there, whatever he may order me to do. If you wish me to keep this wretched life unended by my own hands, help me to get a passage home to England, dear, blessed old England—the very name makes me weep, how bitterly God only knows! You said you would do what you could for me—do this, the last and greatest kindness you can ever do for me, Hereward Pole, if you think the life worth saving of your most miserable, despairing friend,

'JANE.'

This was an appeal to which I could not remain deaf, unless I had had power to change my whole mental constitution. Whatever might be the consequences — and I foresaw

some that were unpleasant, not to say dangerous
and damaging, situated as I was—I was in
honour bound to perform the service required
of me.  Had I not done so, I should have for
ever regarded myself as basely selfish, cold-
hearted, unworthy.  Prudence strongly strove
with me in my cooler moments.  But had I
listened to her dictates, I should ever have
known inwardly that I had consulted my safety,
so to speak, at the expense of every feeling of
manhood, every thought of honour.  I could
not do it.  I wrote at once to the forlorn creature to say that I would do what she wished : in
the meanwhile I counselled prudence, and promised that I would at once take steps to carry
out a plan for her escape, which I sketched out.

It involved, of course, no trifling sacrifice
on my part, but I threw all such considerations
to the winds.  The die was cast.  There was
nothing more to be said.  I immediately set
about my preparations for going down to
Sydney.  Of course I explained matters to the
Major, a preliminary stage which I rather
dreaded.  He heard me with an ominous
silence.  Then he thus delivered himself—

'I don't say you haven't acted generously,

my dear fellow : it was very kind of you, and so on, but women are such confounded fools and so difficult to deal with, particularly when they belong to other people, that I shouldn't like to bet that you won't live to repent your good nature.'

' I shall never do *that*,' I said, 'whatever happens.'

The next thing necessary was to arrange for my journey by coach to Sydney, and, in this respect, fortune appeared to favour me. Mr. Bright, the Bank of New Holland manager, happened to be going down at the same time. He had applied to the Commissioner to go down with the escort, a privilege which was on this occasion graciously extended to me.

' I know you're a good game shot, Pole,' he said. ' I saw you shoot at Windaroo pigeon match when you beat Heathfield. Bring that navy revolver with you, and we shall be a match for all the bushrangers in the country. I always carry a brace of " shooting sticks." '

' That's all very well, but they might take a sitting shot at us, as O'Grady's father did at the sub-sheriff. I'm not so clear that the escort's the best coach after all. There's a deuce of a cargo this time, I hear, and we *might* drop it for "The Brigands of the Black Forest" business.'

'All the better sport,' said the sporting financier. 'They won't catch me napping, I'll be bound. And a bushranger's a better mark than a blue rook, you must admit, Pole.'

'And a better shot too, Captain,' said I. 'I wouldn't mind a ruffle with some of your volunteers, but these fellows mean business when they go on the war-path. However, our passage is taken.'

The first escort that left the Oxley after our claim had washed up was an unusually rich one. Some of the others had taken advantage of the late rains to do likewise. The result was such an aggregation of the 'root of all evil' as sufficed to set most of the unoccupied tongues on the ground wagging. In any other country, perhaps, the transit of twenty-seven thousand ounces of gold, worth more than a hundred thousand pounds sterling, would have excited even more comment. But we had been so much used to seeing bags and parcels, lumps and handfuls of the precious metal handed about in dishes, tin pannikins, and other homely utensils, that we scarcely thought more of it as freight than of so much grain or potatoes.

In the hearts of others, however, there yet lingered, doubtless, covetous feelings and artful schemes more or less feasible as to the illegal appropriation of what we held so lightly, one parcel of which would in foreign lands yield perhaps a life-long term of ease and self-indulgence.

Among the *enfants perdus* of the great mining army were always a score or two of well-known men, always ready to volunteer for a criminal forlorn hope, supposing the prize to be sufficiently tempting.

The occasion of the escort leaving the police camp was one which always involved critical observation and local excitement. In every community there appears to be a distinct class, much of whose time is devoted to the examination of contemporary means of locomotion. They congregate to watch the steamer arrive, the train depart, the coach come in, even the omnibus roll heavily away with unfailing punctuality. At the Oxley the coach arriving bespattered or bedusted after the performance of a long fast journey over bad roads was a daily miracle at which, in despite of a sceptical age, the corps of observation never ceased to marvel. But the gold escort, combining as it did the prestige of a 'stage' with the mystery of a treasure-house, never failed to secure a yet larger and more representative body of spectators.

But that I had reasons of weight for visiting the metropolis at this particular juncture, I should not have quitted my post. I did not like leaving the barque before the anchor was down. I was wise enough to know that any break in a labourer's life makes return to steady work doubly difficult. But I was determined to arrange if possible for the passage to Europe of my old friend and playmate. I wished to save her from the dark fate, the final degradation, in which I had seen others as fair and erst innocent - seeming, engulfed before now. It appeared to me in the light of a sacred duty to my old home life, my old associates. And I was determined to carry it through at all hazards.

On this occasion Mr. Bright and I had from Captain Blake what was esteemed a rare and highly valued privilege on such occasions,

namely, permission to 'travel by the escort,'
as the phrase was, that is, upon the actual
conveyance which carried the treasure-boxes.
Naturally such a permit was not granted indis-
criminately ; but from time to time a banker,
a Government official, or, as in my case, any
resident of the place in whom the Executive
had full confidence, was allowed to take his
seat on the golden chariot.   This equipage
was represented by a strong, heavily - built
American coaching waggon, which, with relays
of four - horse teams, carried rapidly, and in
general safely, the spoils of the alluvial drifts
and quartz ledges.

'By Jove! you are a lucky fellow, Pole,'
said the Commissioner, 'to be able to travel
by Her Majesty's private conveyance with a
thousand ounces of your own gold on board
for pocket-money when you get to town.   I
sometimes think I'll drop the service and take
to digging in good earnest.   What do you say ?
I'm afraid it's too late to buy into No. 4, or
anything on the Sinbad Valley line.   But just
keep your eyes about you, Bright, when you
are passing those confounded Eugowra Rocks.
We've had a whisper that Lardner has been

seen near Yedden Mountain, d—n him! You're
armed, of course?'

I touched my left hip significantly.

'Of course. Too long in the country to
travel unloaded. Bright has his battery, I
know. Well, *bon voyage*. Remember me to
the Chief if you see him. Tell him I'm worked
to death.'  .

A stranger must have augured favourably of
the early habits of the Oxley population who
had witnessed the crowd assembled at five A.M.
at the gate of the camp, at least half an hour
before the departure of the escort. Certainly,
the pure, fresh air of an Australian summer
morn, dominating the stale and sickly odours
of the tawdry bars and empty, dusty streets,
might have seemed to some a sufficient reason.
As the sun rose clear and ruby bright through
the pale eastern pearl fringe, lighting up the
sullen gorge of Eugowra, the frowning, sombre
mountain range, my heart rose as if in unison
with the gracious aspect of Nature, and each
purer, more elevated feeling seemed strength-
ened and exalted. How mysteriously invisible is
the form of coming evil at certain seasons ; how
darkly soul-shrouding its very shadow at others!

On this day, however, success and hope encompassed me, bearing down all doubt and opposition. The Major and Joe came to see us off, and as I passed through the crowd I was sensible of respectful and admiring criticism.

'That's Harry Pole, of No. 4 Liberator, and the best claim on Greenstone, atop of it,' said an old Yatala shepherd, charmed to have the opportunity of explanation. 'Richest claim on the lead, but disputed. Got £20,000 in the bank, and two thousand ounces in that bloomin' escort. Very awkward, ain't it?'

'What's he want to go to town for?' queried a cynical listener. 'What 'ud you or I, mate, want to go to town for, supposin' we washed up once a fortnight to that tune? Wants to have his 'air cut Paris-fashion, or to see the theayter, or leave his card on the Governor-General, may be.'

'Don't they never rob the escort?'

'Well, not much they don't, though I wouldn't say, mind ye, as it mightn't be done by men as 'ud stand a shot for a big touch. They'd have to work it to rights though. Here they come.'

G

At this moment the camp gates were opened, and the well-groomed, high conditioned team, fed with corn that cost a guinea a bushel, and with hay that was much dearer than loaf sugar (it was a dry year and the crops were bad and grass there was none), plunged at their collars, and the heavy but well-hung drag rolled out. The treasure-boxes, to the number of half a hundred or more, were lifted out from Sergeant M'Mahon's room, and counted over carefully to the sergeant in charge of the escort. They were small, compact, and iron-bound, but judging by the way in which they were lifted, remarkably heavy for their size.

On the box sat a senior-sergeant of police, a tall, slight, soldierly-looking man, with a black beard which fell to his breast, and who handled the reins like one to whom such things were familiar. A trooper fully armed, with a Snider rifle between his knees in addition to the navy revolver at his belt, sat beside him. In the body of the drag, where I and Mr. Bright were accommodated with seats, were two more constables similarly armed. A couple of mounted men rode in advance, and as many a short distance behind. The distance was pretty accurately preserved, under all circumstances.  These troopers carried short breechloading carbines.  Well mounted and admirably turned out, as to uniform and equipment—for Mr. Merlin's eye spared no slovenliness of dress on drill—they might have passed muster in any cavalry troop in Europe.

That distinguished official was there, of course, coldly observant, and with such an air of guarded approval as caused every person connected with the equipage and service, from the gold-receiver, Sergeant M'Mahon, to the last pair of mounted troopers, to consider within themselves whether some detail of dress, duty, or deportment had not been left unperformed.

'*Bon voyage*, Bright; good-bye, Pole; good-bye, Harry,' were the last farewells that met my ear from the Major and the crowd.  'Good luck and a jolly trip to you!'  And we were away.

The weather was superb, my companion cheerful and amusing; the roads, though occasionally precipitous, by no means painfully uneven.  The occasion was apparently fortunate.  For a while I fully realised the pleasantness of change and leisure, the cessation of the daily revolution of the gold mill, a machine which becomes as wearisome in time as all other monotonously coercive occupations.

Unconsciously I commenced to dwell upon the still remaining obstacles to the homeward voyage, the contemplation of which, as too feverishly exciting, I always resisted. While at work, it had a tendency to unnerve and unfit for this dull unimaginative frame of dogged endurance which is labour's truest ally. Now I could for a short time revel in the roseate tints and golden haze wherewith the great scene-painter, Fancy, embellishes the dingy properties of life's dull stage.

A few more months' work, a few more washings up at the present most satisfactory rate of yield, No. 4 free from legal hindrances, fairly gone at, and, with the wages-men we could afford to put on, worked out, the vein of auriferous drift would be quickly exhausted. Every square yard of it would be brought to the light of day, puddled, sifted, turned from gravel to minted gold by the rude skill of the miner—that latter-day alchemist.

Then, at last — would Fate permit such
bliss?—I should be in possession of a sum of
at least fifty thousand pounds, perhaps even
more. I should be firmly, indefensibly possessed of that title to respect, which every man
holds who can point to a competence hewn by
his own labour from the sterile, hard, at times
adamantine quarry of labour. I should have
done this almost literally. I should have dis-
proved every word of disparagement that my
enemies could have ever used against me ;
have confirmed the faith of true friends ; have
justified the sublime devotedness of my early
love, my peerless Ruth ; have earned the right
to a future of dignified ease, if not of unalloyed
enjoyment.

In the sophisticated methods of approval
which hold good, in this our day, it may well
be questioned whether a man does not receive
a larger meed of honour and respect who has
been simply the recipient of an ancestral
hoard. Such lands, such wealth, such rank,
represent, ratably, the labour and the
prudence, the valour and the wisdom, it may
well be but the servility or the greed, of the
dead men who have gone before. Their

descendant, by no merit of his own, becomes
the fortunate possessor not only of the lands
and the money-bags ; even by a curious fiction
is credited with the possession of a large share
of the valour and the intellect which he has but
little chance of displaying, and of which it may
be he is wholly devoid. He may never have
done deed or uttered speech which the humblest
labourer on his estate could not have matched.
Yet, in this Pantheon of false gods and outworn
idols, men and women make obeisance yet more
lowly to the puppet of fortune than to the
proved possessor of those qualities by which
families are founded and races are ennobled.

Be this as it might, I had become sufficiently
democratic under my goldfields training to believe that as Hereward Pole, the returned
Australian miner, I should be able to hold
up my head in my own country to some
purpose with the proceeds of No. 4 and the
Greenstone Dyke transmuted into a bank
balance. Even as an unknown adventurer of
fairly decent appearance and manners, with my
trusty cheque-book by my side, that modern
Excalibur, I could hew my way to the notice
of the Queen of the Tournament. But though

few knew, and fewer cared about such a matter
of musty genealogy here, I was none the less
Hereward Pole, a cadet of the ancient house of
Shute, in honour and antiquity second to none
of the companions of the Norman conqueror.

How the days would fly, after I had realised
and gone to town on my final journey to take
my passage by the first mail steamer! What
calm delight to rest from work, even from
thought, long dreamy days, gliding on the
breezeless, languorous Red Sea, or, in glowing
sunset hours, to watch the unresting surge at
play on the long mysterious coast-line of Africa,
ancientest land of wonder and of dread. Past
all mortal visions of happiness would be that
day of days, *should it ever arrive*, ah me! when
the white cliffs, the emerald-green fields of
long-lost, long-loved Albion would greet these
desert-worn eyes!

Then would, indeed, heaven open for me—
here below. Then would that whitest, purely
radiant angel, gazing at me with the well-
remembered, tender-glowing orbs of love——

'Curse that infernal tree—right across the
narrowest bit of the gap! Wonder whether
it blew down, or whether those Yedden Moun-

tain ruffians put it there on purpose ; blank,
blank,' objurgated the sergeant.    'Jump out,
you two, and take the axe ; we might shift it.'

Here was an interruption with a vengeance.
Brought down from realms celestial to this
saddest sordid sphere, where fierce or grovel-
ling passions alternately debase hopeless
humanity.

# CHAPTER XVII

'THERE's something like a gun-barrel behind that spotted gum-tree,' said Mr. Bright, who had dwelt in the bush in his youth, 'and I'll swear I heard a horse stamp. Save your powder and aim low, all of you, whatever you do.'

'Look sharp, men!' growled the sergeant. 'A cross-looking chap, on a black horse, was seen hereabouts yesterday, with another man answering Gilbert Hawke's description. If Darkie and his rider's anywhere handy now, it will be rough work in this beastly gap. Good God! here they are. Close up, men, and defend the escort—steady—fire!'

As the word of command left the sergeant's lips, a volley of firearms resounded, reverberating from each side of the rocky ravine, called The Gap, which we had a short time since entered. At the same time a body of nearly twenty men showed themselves from behind trees and rocks.

I awake—my dream, how rudely shattered —to a full sense of my immediate surroundings. We were attacked by bushrangers. The far-famed pass known as Eugowra Rocks had been picked for the scene of conflict.

This now celebrated spot was on the saddle of a lofty granitic range of hills which inter-sected our road to the metropolis. A tedious ascent led to a spot where the escort coach had just space to wind between the hugh monoliths that reared themselves frowningly in our path. The locality was densely wooded. No element was wanting for our discomfiture. A long stretch of gently descending ground led to the champaign below, where the road was easy and pleasant, without hill or wood to mar the path to the farthest horizon.

We had all been looking forward to this reward of previous anxiety, yet destined never to reach it. All the men were masked and otherwise fully disguised. They had apparently lain in wait in this narrow defile. Now we knew why our progress had been barred. The tree had been felled solely for that purpose.

Our return fire was quicker than they could have calculated upon.   More than one shot told.   It was not the first time I had burned powder in earnest.   Mr. Bright fired as fast and steadily as if he had been engaged in his favourite sport of pigeon-shooting.   There was litttle time for observation, but I thought I recognised a figure that stole from behind a huge rock to take up a nearer position to our ill-fated equipage.

For several minutes, long enough for hours they seemed to me, the fusillade was sharply kept up on either side.   And more than one smothered cry or savage oath told that our ammunition was not all wasted.

The troopers who rode behind had closed up.   Throwing themselves from their horses, and taking what cover they could from the wheels and body of the vehicle, they kept their Terry rifles busy.   But we fought at a disadvantage in every way.   The situation had been carefully calculated.   The immense boulders on either side of the gorge furnished only too complete cover for the attacking party.   Trapped and surprised, we had fallen into an ambuscade laid for us only too successfully.

Debarred from opening out into skirmishing order, we were exposed to a concentrated fire from hidden enemies. They were enabled to take sure and deadly aim at us from behind their more complete defences.

But no man flinched. The troopers—one of whom was a smooth-cheeked youngster, just newly landed in Australia, who had left the paternal rectory but lately for the force, *faute d'autre*—loaded and fired like veterans of the Old Guard.

'That's Malgrade, or the devil,' said I to Mr. Bright, 'he that just slipped behind the rock from the tree. I know his walk, d—n him : no mask can disguise him from *me.*'

'Just what I thought myself,' said Bright; 'let's give it him together, the next time he shows. We ought to nail him between us.'

At the first volley two of our men had dropped, if not mortally wounded, still decidedly *hors-de-combat.* We could not disguise from ourselves that our chance was bad of coming out unscathed or even of successfully defending our precious freight. With every fresh volley one or other was wounded, and every moment the impossibility of long sustaining the unequal fight was felt. Neither could we retreat and carry the gold with us.

Of the good team that had pranced so gaily out of the camp gates this morning one horse lay dead, and the other, badly hit, had broken traces and bolted through the forest. One of the wheelers was unharmed, but the other had two bullets through his body, and though still on his legs was evidently suffering internal agony, as ever and again he turned his eyes plaintively on us and backward to his bleeding flank, as if mutely asking why he should be mixed up in his master's combats.

The escort sergeant had been hit at the first discharge, as indeed had most of us, slightly or otherwise. He, however, held himself straight, and not only fired rapidly himself, but kept the whole of his party well in hand, urging them not to quit cover unnecessarily, but to aim steadily and surely whenever the bushrangers exposed themselves.

'They'll get tired of it if we can only keep them off for another hour,' he said. 'I don't think they care about coming to close quarters. We may get assistance before dark.'

It was not to be. Even as he spoke the

brave fellow's face was changing.  I noticed the
blood staining his blue uniform a bright crimson,
where it welled from his side in heavy, quick-
recurring drops.

They were the last words he ever spoke.
The next moment he swayed for a moment and
fell heavily to the earth.  A cry of exultation
at the fall of our leader rose mockingly amid
the crags, and a rush still nearer was made by
the masked assailants, who now exposed themselves more freely, as if sure of victory.

The man whom I took to be Malgrade
stepped cautiously from behind his rock ; at
that moment Mr. Bright and I fired without a
second's loss of time at his left shoulder.  He
fell, but was dragged behind the rock by some
one, apparently also concealed there, and who
was a taller and broader man than any one we
had as yet noticed.  At the same time the
whole fire of the party poured down upon us,
and both Bright and I felt ourselves wounded
again.

' Only winged, I think,' said Bright, raising
his right arm.  ' Might drop out of bounds, but
I don't think they'll bag me this time.  How
do you feel, Pole ? where are you touched ? '

'Under the rib, and I don't like the feel of it,' said I. 'I wonder if we drilled that scoundrel Malgrade, if it *was* him. By Jove, that young Rowan's done.'

Two troopers lifted up the poor youngster, shot through the body and apparently dying.

'We can do nothing by stopping here, Mr. Bright,' said the second in command, a grizzled, sun-burned senior constable, who looked as if he had seen much service. 'We shall all get potted and not save the gold either; that's what I look at. The best thing is to retreat across to that scrub alongside of Stony Pinch. I know a track down it. I don't think they will follow us there.'

'Leaving the ship while there's a plank to stand on is devilishly mean work,' said Bright, blazing away in quick succession as he spoke, 'but I suppose we can't do any good this time. The sergeant's stone dead, poor fellow; that youngster's little better, and Pole here doesn't look as if he'd hold out long. I suppose we can take the horses and retreat in good order?'

'We can manage that,' said the senior constable. 'They only want the gold, blast them; and the sooner we get the black trackers on the

trail, then the sooner we shall have a chance of
seeing some of it back.'

So, keeping our faces to the foe and main-
taining a brisk fire, we commenced to retreat
slowly, leading the unwounded horses and carrying the young trooper with us. As soon as it
was seen that we had given up trying to defend
the gold, no attempt was made to follow us up.
Doubtless, it was thought that in our desperation we should not prove less formidable than at
present.

One man only among the bushrangers had
any personal animosity to gratify. This was
Malgrade, if, indeed, it was as I supposed.
And he had apparently received his quietus for
a time. A few dropping shots followed us as
we made our way slowly and with difficulty
through the forest, which commenced to become
more dense until it ended in a perfect thicket,
or what to Australians is known as a scrub.

Here we struck after a while into a narrow,
well-worn path, which led down a steep rocky
defile, tortuously but distinctly. In less than a
couple of miles we debouched upon a comparatively level and thickly-grassed meadow or creek
flat. Here it was proposed that we should rest,

while the senior constable, who knew the country well, rode across to the nearest police station, whence the tidings could be at once sent to the Oxley, and half a hundred other headquarters. No time would be lost in setting a brace of black trackers on the trail of the robbers, who no doubt would have expended no unnecessary time in clearing out with the treasure. Assistance would, of course, be sent to us without a moment's delay.

The trooper dashed off on the best horse of the party, within three minutes of our halt, leaving us in the gathering twilight in no very enviable position. As fast falling shades of night commenced to gather around, the darksome trees which fringed the creek, the gliding waters which murmured along its channel, the heavy hanging cliffs of the dimly outlined mountain, gained a weird and melancholy tone. Our feelings were closely in unison with the solitary scene, the closing day. They could hardly be otherwise than mournful. We had started in the morning full, if not of high hope, of that cheerful confidence in the future which is born of untried dangers, untempted perils. The gold which we bore with us was pleasantly

connected with our tools and avocations. The
day was bright, the journey little more than a
pleasure excursion.

Now how darkly, how irrevocably all was
changed! A dead man and dying horses lay
beside the stranded carriage which had borne us
forth so gaily in the morning. Stiff with our
wounds, hungry, cold, and weary, our attitudes
were gloomy and despairing. The pale countenance of the wounded man, streaked with
blood, looked more ghastly in the flickering
light of the fire which one of the others had at
length lighted.

Is it a heated imagination, or are there other
forms, strange shadows, gliding around the
watch-fire and amid the dark-leaved water-oaks?
They gather around upon the wounded man,
whose laboured breathing I seem to hear with
ever-increasing distinctness.

'Bright, I say, Bright! don't let those
people crowd so closely round Rowan, they
will smother him. Good God! do you not
hear?'

'Your head must be going, Pole,' said the
banker seriously, who was sitting on a log
smoking resignedly and watching the wounded

man. 'Come over and let me see where they touched you. Take care——'

But I hear no more. I rise and stagger blindly forward, and the blood pours from my side. I see a crowd of spectres hurrying towards me—my head swims, and my eyes are darkened as in death.

When I recovered my senses I was lying under a tree in the cool moonlight, with Bright bending anxiously over me. All was over now, it seemed to me.

How joyously had I marked the sun rise over this very mountain, as I rose from my humble couch at Yatala. And now the same orb had but set, and with it the sun of Hereward Pole's fortune. What a satiric comment on man's vain life and vainer hopes! All was gone — hope and fortune, love, gold, and life itself ; and here I lay under this darksome forest tree with the life-blood fast ebbing away, and scarce a trace would be left of a wasted existence, blighted career.

Well, the news would soon reach Allerton Court ; the country busybodies would be enabled to verify their long-cherished foreboding that nothing would come of my gold-seeking adven-

ture, and that everything had turned out exactly
as they expected from the very first day of the
Squire's sanction to his daughter's ridiculous
engagement.

Then I died! Can a man die more than
once? Is it not a real death when the flickering senses first dwindle down to the lowest
point of consciousness? Men arouse themselves as at a faintly-heard summons once more
to animate the sinking frame, in pain and mutest
agony, clinging with the might of despair to
every last buttress of the ruined citadel. Then
an appalling sense of general departure from
this long-accustomed mortal tenement joined
with a mysterious boding horror of undefined
doom. A time of coldness, numbness, deadly
still-creeping paralysis over the centre of sensation—then utter darkness—extinction.

.    .    .    .    .    .

It would appear that I had not finally quitted
this lower earth; for I reopened my eyes yet
again. They rested not upon satanic or celestial
personages other than Mr. Inspector Merlin,
who was sitting by my bedside in an attitude of
(for him) great patience and amiability.

He rose quickly to his feet with a sigh of

relief, remaining silent for a short space so as
apparently to enable me to realise the fact that
I was in a rude but neatly-furnished slab cottage,
accommodated with all the comforts which a
small farmhouse could furnish.  Then he spoke—

'Well, Pole, old man, you're worth a brace
of dead men yet—a near thing, though.  The
doctor said that a shade closer to the main
artery, and you would have been gathered to
your strong-minded ancestor the Legate.  Now
you've got such a good-looking, neat-handed
nurse to look after you, you're sure to come
out right.'

'What has become of the other—fellows,
and—the gold?' said I feebly.  'Who stuck
us up?'

'Why, Frank Lardner, of course, b—t
him!' said Mr. Merlin with perhaps allowable
anger.  'We know that Wall, Gilbert Hawke,
and Daly were with him, besides half a dozen
other ruffians of less note.  Sergeant Webber
is dead and buried; Constable Rowan not
expected to live.  Watson has got a bullet in
his hip, and will be lame for life.  Bright was
winged, and not much the worse for it.  The
gold was all taken of course, but the "wire"

brought a cordon of police round them within twelve hours, and we know they can't have got clear off with it. We have great hope of recovering the lot within a month.'

'Thank God for that,' I said. 'I ought perhaps to think of my life first; but if all the gold was gone I shouldn't think the other very valuable. And so it was Master Frank, was it, with Wall, Gilbert Hawke, and the rest? What a pity such smart fellows should have taken to the bush and commenced with such a cold-blooded murderous outrage.'

'Pity,' said Merlin, drawing his lips slightly back, and showing his white teeth in a way which reminded me of the jaguar aroused. 'I'd find them pity if I saw them at the end of a half-inch line; and by —— you will see them there one day, as sure as my name's Mainwaring Merlin. Think of poor Webber, what a fine fellow he was! I shall never get such another accountant either,' he added reflectively. 'By God! I could hang them with my own hands. And now I must be off. Mrs. Morton, or whatever you call her, will be here directly. I quite envy you.'

Here Mr. Merlin took himself off, and went

on the war-path, which indeed he had seldom
quitted by night or by day since the terrible
news of the Great Escort Robbery.  Tireless,
pitiless, even at the highest pitch of energy and
alertness in mind and body, he was a dangerous
enemy for the Yedden Mountain gang, as they
were called, to arouse, and so indeed they found
it before all was done.  Had I been strong
enough to smile, I must have done so at the
*naïveté* of his regret for poor Sergeant Webber,
whose clerkly qualities, plucky and clever officer
as he was in other respects, mainly endeared
him to Mr. Merlin's organising soul.

The sound of his footsteps had hardly died
away when the rustle of a woman's dress told
me that the nurse of whom he spoke was
approaching.  Strange was it that something,
even in that symbolical token of woman's
presence, brought back to me a memory of the
long-vanished past.  But I had taxed my
strength too much.  Falling helplessly back
upon the pillow, I fainted.  I had a dim,
confused recollection of feeling my forehead
bathed, of the tender touch of a woman's hand
passing lightly over it, of a cordial held to my
lips.  With a painful effort I raised my head

and opened my eyes. I could hardly trust the evidence of my senses. I thought I must be wandering again, and that I fancied myself at Dibblestowe Leys; for the face which was bending over me, full of womanly tenderness, was the face of Jane Mangold.

I saw again the bright blue eyes, the soft fair hair, the delicate features of her who, before my knowledge of Ruth Allerton, had been to me the embodiment of fairest womanhood. At the first glance she seemed unchanged. Then I marked with pain the deepened lines in her face, the saddened brow, the worn anxious look, which had replaced the girlish defiant expression which I had always associated with her laughing eyes and saucy smile. The sad handwriting which the world and its pitiless warfare inscribes upon its victims was there indelibly imprinted.

'Jane,' I said, 'dear Jane, are we both at the Leys again; or how do I see you here? Ah, why did you come to me?'

'How could I help coming to nurse you, when I heard you were dying?' she said. 'Have you not been a friend—a brother to me? Have you not saved me from what is

worse than death? And am I to do nothing
for you to show my gratitude? Mr. Merlin
told me your life might depend upon careful
nursing.'

All this she uttered in her old quiet way of
speaking when anything moved her more than
common. Once more vividly real, under the
shadow of death. How the old life career came
back to me!

'But, Jane,' I said, 'people will talk, and
you know at Yatala it does not take long——'

'If I am to be the cause of shame and
disgrace to you, I will go away and hide my
wretched self the moment you have recovered
from your wound. It shall never be said that
I helped to harm you—you who have been
better than a brother; but the doctor says,
even now, that you may not get over it. And
I thought that she, that Miss Allerton, might
be glad to know that a friendly hand, even if it
was poor Jane Mangold's, helped to do what
only a woman can for a man at the last.' Here
she buried her head in her hands and wept
unrestrainedly.

'You are right, Jane,' I said, 'and I will
answer for my dearest Ruth, that she will be

grateful to you, if I see her face no more, for smoothing my pillow before the last sleep. We have always been friends, why should we not be true to each other to the last ? Let us keep faith with ourselves and the absent, and the world may say its say.'

She raised herself and looked wistfully at me.

'I only know that I should be glad if I were in her place,' said she, 'and would thank on my knees any one that did for my lover what I will do for you in your hour of need.'

Here I could no longer support the fatigue of conversation, and, for a space, again 'effaced myself.'

# CHAPTER XVIII

This affair, of course, created an immense sensation, not only in the immediate neighbourhood of the Oxley rush, but throughout Australia. Certain lawless acts and deeds had been committed on all diggings. We were not, as communities, entirely free from crime, although, as I have attempted to describe, the average of serious offences against life and property was certainly lower than in many settlements of older date and higher pretensions to civilisation. But now any delusion as to the gradually improving tendency of the race was rudely dispelled.

A new, startling, and flagrant outrage had been committed. The affair had been arranged with laborious foresight. The details had been carried out with only too great elaboration. The result was complete and successful. Her

Majesty's servants and lieges had been shot
down in cold blood. The escort, always intimately associated with Government guarantee
and protection, had been captured. Hard-
working miners had been despoiled of their
well-earned gold. And by whom had this
been done? By whom planned, by whom
carried out? Not by the fierce desperadoes of
other climes, the probable outcome of piracies
on the Spanish Main, of murders in Sonora, or
gambling in the hells of San Francisco, but by
'sons of the soil,' as political patriotism forcibly expressed the fact, by men reared amid
the forest-farms of the interior, who in their
youth had been peaceful stockmen and station-
labourers, who had followed the flocks or hunted
the wild horse from boyhood, amid the streams
and gullies of that very Yedden Mountain
which rose dark and as if frowningly in the
sight of the scene. It was to the philanthropist
a grievous and discouraging fact, to the
pessimist an unholy triumph. Well might the
poet deprecate the *auri sacra fames.* Better
hopes hitherto had been entertained. But now
the country was obviously going to perdition ;
the men and women reared therein would be

basely degenerate from a race whose flag the
world had been forced to fear in war and
respect in peace for a thousand years.

Such were the reflections of many honest
Australian citizens, who deplored as deeply the
nationality of the criminals as the criminality of
the deed.   In the meantime all imaginable steps
were taken for the capture of the outlaws and
the recovery of the treasure.   With this latter
attempt greater success was reached than with
the former.   So complete was the cordon with
which the robber band was surrounded, so
ceaseless the vigilance that left no hour of the
day or night free from tireless tracking and
close pursuit, that the heavily laden pack-horses
with which they had commenced the transport
of the gold boxes were abandoned, and the
larger portion of the original gold recovered.

Among the treasure-trove lay, fortunately,
sealed and accurately labelled, as were all the
separate parcels, the leathern bag which con-
tained the contribution of Greenstone Dyke,
addressed to Mr. Hereward Pole, Bank of New
Holland, Sydney; so that with the somewhat
serious deduction of 'a vision of sudden death,'
a gunshot wound hard by a vital spot, consider-

able loss of time, money, and peace of mind, matters in a few weeks would be much as they had been before my departure for Sydney.

But the capture of the band of outlaws was not so soon accomplished. Of all outlaws, the Australian bushranger has proved the most difficult to secure after a series of crimes has rendered him desperate.

' Native, and to the manner born,' he possesses natural advantages amid the wilds and fastnesses of the interior, with which the officials of the law find it difficult, in some cases impossible, to contend. A horseman of matchless skill and daring from childhood, with the best blood in England, ay, even of the desert, often at his control, he is the equal of the Apache or the Comanchee in the saddle, their superior in strength and courage. In the broken and mountainous country near which he is generally concealed, he has the advantage of scouts of unrivalled activity and acuteness. These ' bush telegraphs,' as the modern robber slang has dubbed them, are of all avocations and both sexes.

The brown-faced urchin lounging after his father's cows on a three-legged screw, with a

ragged saddle and green-hide girth, fixes his
watchful half-savage eyes upon the troopers as
they enter the forest and disappear up the winding slate-strewed ravine. They wear rough
tweed suits and old felt hats; they are riding
on stockmen's saddles with rusty stirrup-irons.
But *he* knows them for all that, and marks them
down unerringly. The bare-legged girl tending
the small flock of sheep, or racing after the
milker's calves, meets the strange horsemen then
camped by a creek, and demurely answers their
questions as to strayed bullocks. She knows
'the traps' by a dozen signs visible to the
initiated. And at midnight or before dawn the
robber in the traditional cave or the dismal
deserted hut knows that the avengers of blood
are on his trail, and flees noiselessly as the night-
hawk to yet more secluded haunts.

How should they be run down, surrounded,
or surprised? Well armed, well mounted, fearless horsemen, and for the most part quick-eyed
and keen of hearing as the hunted deer before the
questing hound; strong in desperate need, and
brave with the demoniac feeling that liberty and
life have been forfeited irrevocably, small wonder
that the latter-day bushrangers of the Australian

continent have, ere now, for months and even years defied the concentrated efforts of the respectable portion of the community to arrest or exterminate them. Such bands have for months, even longer periods, sufficed to keep a whole country-side in a constant state of peril and anxiety. Appearing here on a given day, robbing the mail, and parading every traveller on a certain line of road with almost ludicrous impartiality—within forty-eight hours besieging an isolated station, or robbing a bank two hundred miles away.

After more weary days Dr. Winthrop, who had ridden hundreds of miles in my case alone, at length thought I was well enough to be moved.

'By Jove! Harry, a narrow squeak,' he said; 'if the bullet had been from a navy revolver instead of one of those Derringer toys, it would have made all the difference. Couldn't have gone a thread closer without rupturing the cœliac axis. Mrs. What's-her-name here has nursed you admirably. Old friend of yours, she says. Helped to save you as much as anything. Very pretty woman she is too. What's she going to do now she's left that brute her husband?'

'Going home to her friends in England, and so you can tell any one that takes an interest in my affairs,' I said, rather stiffly.

'Quite right, quite right, glad to hear it,' said the doctor. 'People *will* talk, you know, especially at the diggings. Glad to know there's no foundation, etc. Yarns get about. So the sooner you're back at your own camp the better. I'll tell the Major or Bulder they can drive over for you any day. A mattress laid on one of those light American traps wouldn't shake you much. I suppose you heard about Merlin's men picking up the pack-horse, with ever so many gold-bags—Greenstone Dyke lot all right among them, and so on.'

'I did hear of it,' I said languidly. 'Caught any of the gang yet?'

No, confound them, and not likely to. The police are worked off their legs. Though they've been very near them once or twice, they've always got off. Been sticking up people and places all over the country; might catch me as I go back—no knowing. They're never hard on the learned professions though. Sure to want them all some day. Good-bye, Harry.'

The day after this conversation Joe Bulder
arrived with a quiet horse and light tray buggy,
the movable seat of which had been taken out.
A mattress with all requirements in the shape
of feather pillows, etc., contributed by a lady
neighbour and Mrs. Yorke (for Cyrus had come
over to work my share, and his wife refused to
remain) was placed therein. With Joe's help
and that of Jane I was able with great difficulty,
pale, tottering, and death-like, feeble as I was,
to stretch myself on my improvised ambulance.
Jane sat by my side, while Joe walked by the
horse's head, and patiently led the animal with
a careful avoidance of all inequalities in the
road.

'Yon's a queer start,' he said, after a long
pause. 'If some of the folk at the Leys could
see us three now, they'd think all the gold in
Jewellers' Point wouldn't ha' tempted them to
cross seas. When word coomed as you was
killed along o' the sergeant and all the escort
clean gutted, I felt loike as though I'd never
stay another day in the land. I offered my
share to Mr. Olivera for ten thousand down,
and I'd ha' been off back next mail sure as
there's hops in Kent. Dang the country and

the people too. I'm nigh sick on it all. I
could wish, loike some folk says, I'd never
seen it.'

Jane gave a deep, half-unconscious sigh.

Joe had relapsed into his provincial dialect,
as he generally did in moments of excitement,
and doubtless failed for a short time to realise
the very decided advance of his personal and
pecuniary position, maugre even such adventures
as gunshot wounds, escort robberies, and
revolutions.

' Never mind, Joe, the battle's not over yet,'
I said. ' It's not like an Englishman to jack
up and give these fellows best. We'll see some
of these fellows hanged yet—those that are not
shot, I mean. And talking of being hanged,
was that fellow Malgrade at the township when
the news came ? '

' Nay, that he was na,' replied Joe, looking
surprised, 'for a man I know told me as he
should go to his camp to borrow a long-handled
shovel early that morning. They was both
away, he and his mate too ; yon long chap, as
he always called Harry, him with the big
whiskers. This man tells me they didn't get
back till nine o'clock ; more than that, Harry's

big bay horse was knocked up, and Malgrade's hadn't no more than a crawl in him. They'd come a goodish step by that'n, and no mistake.'

'How do you know, Joe?'

'Why, you see, Malgrade's horse is a bit of blood—only on the cross like himself; he's won a good many races on the sly like, droppin' in at country meetings on the quiet, and always in condition, and big Harry has been a cattle-stealer, every one says. He's a heavy weight, but yon bay horse of his can carry him like as he was a schoolboy. They'd ridden no twenty mile that night, nor fifty neither, it's my thinkin'.'

'Had they anything with them?'

'Not as he could see. Malgrade had a poncho on, and might have carried a bushel bag inside without any one being the wiser. But they didn't want to talk. Malgrade had a stiff arm—said his nag had fell with him and chucked him ont' the shovel, and he went off, as he was late for his work.'

'I'll lay my life both those fellows were in the robbery. I have a kind of recollection of a tall man on a big bay horse in the confusion, but of course they were all masked.'

'They'd both rob a church, it's my opinion
of 'em,' said Joe, 'and Malgrade wouldn't stick
at cutting the priest's throat after if there was
aught to be made of it.   As for big Harry, he's
an old pal of all those Yedden Mountain boys,
for I've heard him say as much.'

'If you talk any more you'll undo all my
nursing,' said Jane with a wistful look, 'and you
*do* want to see the Leys again, and—another
place, Hereward, *don't* you?'

When I found myself back at the tent at
the Oxley things looked much as usual.   Indeed
the passing wave of excitement consequent on
'the unparalleled outrage,' as the *Beacon* for
once truly characterised the late occurrence,
had long subsided.   Events of considerable
magnitude are so quick and recurrent in large
mining centres that, as human nature is constituted, the mental expense of prolonged interest is too great to be borne.   So having well
digested the facts, stupendous as they might
have appeared in an old-world place like the
Leys, that the escort had been robbed, police-
men shot, the gold carried off and partly recovered, Harry Pole, of No. 4 Liberator, and
Greenstone, badly hurt, and the bushrangers

still at large, eating and drinking, work and play, digging and dicing, litigation and love-making, crushing and washing up, were all being eagerly transacted at the Oxley, much as though nothing had ever happened contrary to the ordinary course of life.

Jane was temporarily located with Mrs. Yorke, and Cyrus bidden by his wife to betake himself to the nearest hotel for the present.

'There'll have to be some one to nurse Harry for a good month to come,' said that matron, 'and I've not got the time to do it, though I'd be willing enough, as he knows; but the cooking and the washing and the children's quite enough for one woman these short days. Jane had better keep with me till Harry's about again. She won't do me no harm, poor thing, and my belief is she'd have been straight enough only for that brute of a husband of hers. Of course us poor women are blamed for everything. But what's going to come of her when this hole through your poor side's mended, Harry? She can't live here for ever. There'll be a lot of yarns about it as it is.'

'Of course, she will go home to her friends

in England, Mrs. Yorke. I was going to see about a ship for her this time, if I hadn't been stopped. It's very kind of you to have her here, I know. You may take my word for it that everything will be done for her by me that a man could do for his sister. We're old friends, you know ; and a man may have a true friendship for a countrywoman in her distress, I should hope.'

'Oh yes, I suppose so,' said Mrs. Yorke, a little doubtfully, 'not that I hold with running it too fine ; when folks is young, and one of 'em that pretty as people in the street turn round to look at her, partic'lar on the diggings, where there's a lot of curious women. Anyway, my character ain't to be shook that easy, not if I was to take in worse than her for a spell. But I've known you, Harry Pole, these years, so I'll take your word that everything's on the square, and Cyrus says the same.'

'Thank you very much, Mrs. Yorke, you may trust me. I hope I shall soon cease to be a bother to any one. And now tell me some of the news. None of these scoundrels caught yet ?'

'Not a half a one. The p'leece is doing

their best night and day, nothing but telegrams
and camping out and half killing themselves
and their horses.  Merlin's lamed his old gray
horse, and got an awful cold, and is that savage
no one durst speak to him.  Malgrade met him
one day, though, in the street.'

'Ha! what did he say?'

'Oh, he stops as cool as you please, and says,
"Good morning, Mr. Merlin, may I ask if you
have any news of the escort robbers?"

'"The ruffians are neither shot nor taken
yet, Mr. Malgrade," and he looks as if his eyes
was gimlets and would bore two holes right
through him in no time.  "I believe they
receive intelligence from meaner villains than
themselves who probably shared the plunder
without the danger.  I have reason to think
there are men on this field even now that ought
to be arrested on suspicion."

'Malgrade looked just as straight at him,
Cyrus says, you'd have thought he was the
honestest man in the world.  Then he smiles
a bit and shows his white teeth.

'"Indeed," he says, "how very interesting.
No doubt you will get them all in time.  Good
morning."

'And he walks down the street as if the Banks belonged to him.'

'Then Merlin suspects him?'

'Of course he does; he and big Harry was in it up to their necks, the diggers all say. But there's no evidence, and I suppose law's law. Yankee Tom says if they'd been where he's been they'd have been "lynched" afore now.'

'That's all very well,' I rejoin, 'when you're quite sure of the right man. But it's awkward if mistakes are made. British law is the best and fairest, and quite generally reaches far enough in the long-run.'

'Well, it ought to be sure, for it's awful slow at times; and if we lose No. 4 I ll never believe in law nor justice again as long as I live. However, this claim's shaping first-rate now. All you've got to do is to get on your legs again, and we'll all have enough to keep us without soiling our hands for the rest of our lives, if every other man round Murderers' Flat was a bushranger, and I don't believe they're much better.'

'All's well that ends well, Mrs. Yorke— which means that a good "washing-up" will fetch everything straight. We must trust in the Oxley " dirt " and a kind Providence.'

My wound, thanks to the tender tireless nursing of poor Jane, and the treatment of one of the cleverest surgeons in the southern hemisphere—a man well-nigh faultless, so that you could keep brandy from him and him from brandy—healed apace. Three months only had passed since the day when, with darkening eyes and flowing blood from a mortalseeming wound, I was dimly conscious that our gold was in the hands of the spoiler.

Short seemed the interval, yet how had the great healer, Time, amended our lot. My hurt was as good as cured. I felt almost as well as ever. And the gold was all restored but a trifle of ten thousand ounces, hidden to this day. But Sergeant Webber lay quiet in his grave, and near him the young trooper, Rowan, poor, plucky, bright-eyed boy, not a year from England.

For a while now a season of unusual quietude seemed to have set in at the Oxley. There were no wars or rumours of wars as far as were known to us. The bushrangers certainly were not yet captured, but they did not again molest

our district, and were beginning to wax faint as
impressions on men's minds.   My full strength
returned and I found myself soon as well fitted
as ever to do my work and enjoy 'God's
glorious oxygen' again.

The washings-up were frequent and flourish-
ing.   Our credit balance mounted to a most
respectable figure in the books of the Bank of
New Holland.   From time to time we saw
Jane (who had resolutely refused to rejoin her
husband) when she came out from her retire-
ment to have a talk to Mrs. Yorke, by whose
children she was held to be a beneficent fairy.

Having made so indifferent a start on this
ever-memorable occasion, it was only natural
that I should postpone my next visit to the
metropolis.   The game was patently not worth
the candle if one was liable to the trifling risk
of losing one's gold and being shot through the
body afterwards.   So I decided to stay quietly
at my work until Christmas-time at least, then
five or six months distant, and go down by
Cobb and Co.'s coach in regular orthodox
fashion.

Then the question of Jane Mangold (I
never could call her by any other name) was

a difficult one to settle.  She took a lodging in
the town, at an inn kept by a very decent
kindly widow, who allowed her the free use
of her own private parlour, and in every way
maternised her.  But it was a dismal, unsatisfactory mode of life.  She resolutely refused to
make other acquaintances, male or female,
secluding herself as much as possible, and
only appearing on such occasions as were
necessary for her health.  A blameless sequestered life in every sense was hers.  Still we
thought it unnecessary that our friendly intercourse should be altogether broken off.  I was
her only friend, and from time to time we
indulged ourselves in conversation and harmless friendly intercourse.  I promised her also
that she should follow me down to Sydney
when I went at Christmas-time, when I would
make all arrangements for her passage and see
her on board ship myself.

'Oh, if you would!' she said.  'Sorry as I
should be to see your face no more, still I should
feel so utterly free from all care and anxiety—
so uplifted to a region of bliss, if I were once
fairly on board ship, homeward bound—that I
could almost die for pure joy.'

'And that joy you shall have, Jane,' I said,
'as sure as Christmas comes and we both live.
I will not leave till you are safe on board and
the vessel sailing.   So have no further care in
the matter.   It is only four months now.'

'But it is so much trouble,' she sobbed, 'and
my passage money will be an expense to you.
How shall I ever thank you, my only friend in
this sore need ?'

'Where should I have been if you had not
looked after me at Eugowra ?' I said jokingly.
'Why, the doctor told me that nothing but
your good nursing pulled me through.   You
have saved my life, remember.'

'And you have given me mine in return,'
she said passionately.   'A new life, a true and
pure one henceforth, I swear to you, one that
the angels will not blame when my hour comes.
Always remember that, Hereward Pole ; and
may the good deed bring you the happiness
you deserve, if ever man did, in the future.'

'But, Jane,' I said——

She lifted her hand with a rapid gesture of
farewell—and was gone.

# CHAPTER XIX

In the tiny forest-shaded pools, in lonely mountain tarns or stilly meres, amid placid restful surroundings, the influence of the fallen stone or branch agitates the surface for comparatively long protracted periods. The unwonted disturbance is succeeded by a series of ripples in ever-widening circles until the gazer marvels when the lakelet will subside into pristine unruffled calm. But in the roaring flood-tide of great rivers, or on the turbulent bosom of the mighty main, fleets with whole crews may disappear, or argosies laden with the treasures of Ind be whelmed with scarce a momentary displacement.

So in the wide and complicated goldfields society, had even my life fallen forfeit to the robber's aim, short would have been the moan made, and brief the requiem sung for me at the

Oxley.   The tribute of respect and regret would have been sincere if transitory.   A day's cessation of labour would have been ordered at many a claim, doubtless.   A long procession of vehicles in all grades, horsemen and foot, would have followed Hereward Pole, a brother miner deceased, to the often-visited cemetery under the pine-covered hill.   But that duty well and truly performed, a few rough expressions of sorrow, a few extra glasses to the memory of a comrade 'gone where we all must go,' and the circumstance would be dismissed, myself almost as utterly forgotten as if I had never been.

What wonder then that even the still uncaptured band of bushrangers, *question ardente* as it was, commenced to lose novelty and interest.

The public were evidently beginning to think the piece had enjoyed too long a run, and that the management should bestir themselves to replace the tragedy with a genuine novelty.

That desired melodrama was already forward in rehearsal, if we had but known it, and the leading actors were becoming so perfect in their parts that the rise of the curtain bade fair to be demanded at no distant date.

In the early days of mining, when great yields

of gold were freely won from the shallow alluvial
deposits, a great influx of Chinese had taken
place.   These aliens, for the most part harmless
and industrious, became stubborn and rebellious
as their numbers made them formidable.

To the European miners, apart from their
legitimate competition, they became especially
distasteful.   Their filthy habits when congregated in large camps prevented all ordinary
residents from living in their vicinity.   They
swarmed over the alluvial diggings directly gold
was found, monopolising the auriferous tracts.
At the same time they rarely prospected for
themselves.

For a year past the great body of miners had
been sullenly enduring rather than acquiescing
in this state of matters.   The Commissioner
had no love for the Mongolian or other dark-
skinned aliens ; still they were all equal before
the law, and as long as each man could produce
his talisman in the shape of a Miner's Right, he
strictly enforced his privilege as against the
most popular and influential miner on the field.
He had, indeed, privately represented at headquarters that the rapid absorption of newly-
discovered alluvial tracts by these swarming

aliens would sooner or later lead to an *émeute*. He had gone so far as to suggest that they should only be permitted to work the abandoned portions of the gold areas, where their patient and frugal habits always secured them ample returns.

As before remarked, they were distasteful to the Commissioner, and one morning I had reason to note the Captain's autocratic acts and deeds. I had called early at the camp on some matter of mining business, when the Commissioner, who was always afoot soon after daybreak, whatever had been the carousals of the previous night, espied me and insisted that I should breakfast with him. At that time the camp resembled a military mess, at which, besides the ordinary mining officials, there were sure to be a few strange guests, tourists, with perhaps a surveyor or other members of the Civil Service on leave. Blake's hospitality was unbounded, and a good cook was often available from among the crowd of wanderers who made their temporary home at the Great Rush.

So I cheerfully complied, and a very merry meal it was, save for one incident, which bordered on the tragic and might have been

funereal.  It would seem that his mightiness
the Lord High Commissioner had been annoyed
by the intrusion of certain irreverent miners upon
the grounds immediately in front of the official
residence.  They had made a short cut to a
dam on the creek, and the sight of all kinds of
'fossickers' and such small deer trampling across
the sacred enclosure commenced to irritate our
Czar.  He immediately issued a ukase disal-
lowing such trespass, and caused a notice to be
affixed to the largest gum-tree at the entrance
of the forbidden path.

Chatting carelessly, some one made an in-
cautious remark reflecting upon the courage of
his kangaroo dogs, a grand-looking, wiry-haired
pair, which looked as though they might be
'black St. Hubert's breed.'  This nettled our
host, who was passionately attached to his dogs.
He then and there swore that there was not
only no old man kangaroo in the land that Ban
and Buscar would not tackle, but they would go
at any living thing that he (Blake) chose to set
them on.  A few moments after this slight *contretemps* I saw his brow suddenly corrugate as
he fixed his eyes upon the entrance to the path
about which the late order had arisen.

We all looked, and waited the explosion.
There, sure enough, were two Chinamen,
heavily laden with pans, picks, and other
mining implements, essaying to pass on. They
looked for a moment with stolid faces at the
warning placard, but, less enlightened than Mr.
Jingles's historical pointer, dismissed the subject
with customary ' no savey,' and clambered over
the fence.

' Good God!' exclaimed Blake, with his brow
as black as thunder. 'Am I never to be left
in peace? Here, Wharton, Somers, Hayward,
where are you all?' he roared out. 'See those
infernal Chinamen—I'll teach them a lesson.
Loose the dogs!'

The police troopers, who dwelt generally at
the rear—his orderly and another or two—
knowing from experience that when the Captain
was in one of his moods he brooked no delay,
ran at once to the kennel and opened the door,
when not only Ban and Buscar aforesaid, but
half a score of the other big greyhounds, came
teeming out through the house like a canine
avalanche on hearing their master's voice.

' Hold 'em, boys, hold 'em!' shouted Blake,
and with one glance round the eager dogs

dashed into speed, and sighting the luckless
Celestials, by this time nearly through the
enclosure, made for them as if they had been
a brace of stray 'foresters' from the adjacent
ranges.

The shouting had apparently only just
reached the ears of the doomed ones, for they
turned inquiringly, when, catching sight of the
eager hounds stretching out, open mouthed,
directly in their tracks, they dropped their loads,
and with a yell of affright made for the high
fence at the outlet.

Before they could reach it the swifter
savage brutes were upon them. Both men
were down and apparently half worried before
we could do more than start hurriedly to their
rescue.

'By Jove,' said Blake, picking up his hunting
crop, 'this looks serious. Run, boys, all of you,
or that brute Buscar will have the throat out of
his man.'

We did our best, I need not say; but just
as we got up, one man, rising to his feet, broke
through the pack, climbed up to the top of the
fence, with bleeding limbs and nearly every
rag torn off him, and stood there yelling con-

tinuously in tones that might have been heard
at Sailor's Gully, five miles off.  As for the
other poor fellow, old Smoker and Ban were
dragging him along the ground by the arm, Ban
with red jaws that showed he had found something other than cotton or silk to tear.

The troopers charged desperately with us in
a body, and carried off both the men to the
camp before the crowd of diggers which had
begun to assemble could interfere.

'No harm done, "boys,"' said Blake,
addressing them with his humorous audacity,
which always stood him in good stead; 'only a
couple of Chinamen that couldn't read plain
English, and I sent the dogs over to translate
it to them.  The big man was in luck that
Smoker gripped his arm instead of his throat.
His jacket was mighty well padded, for it
tangled the poor fellow's teeth.'

The crowd laughed and dispersed; and
although the *Beacon* was loud on the 'man and
a brother' question, nothing more came of it.
Blake's sharp eye had discovered that the
assaulted Chinamen, having lately arrived, were
habited in garments thickly padded with cotton,
which prevented the serious damage which

might otherwise have taken place ; only an ugly laceration of the muscles of the arm showed where Smoker's sharp teeth had at length penetrated, but nothing more than the doctor speedily set right. And when Sing Foo and Chong Mow left the camp that evening with considerably more strong waters on board than they were in the habit of taking, each with a new suit of clothes and a couple of sovereigns of the Captain's money, the younger and less injured individual of the two was heard to express himself thus—

'Welly good man Captain Blake—welly bad dog.　All litee.'

If the whole Chinese question could have been settled as promptly by the Commissioner and his dogs, much anxiety on the part of the Government, and, indeed, both blood and treasure might have been saved. *Dis aliter visum.*

Blake had in truth long foreseen the danger. He had drafted a series of regulations by the adoption of which all dissatisfaction might have been removed and subsequent evils prevented. Ever decisive and clear-headed, he would have cut the Gordian knot, as events proved, had a larger measure of discretionary power been allotted to him after his report went in.

It is in the nature of all great moral outbursts that minor matters should prepare the way previously.  The fuel is laid, the combustive forces are gradually generated, the contact of metallic substance is alone wanting; supplied through apparently fortuitous agency, the rending explosion follows, and the volcano bursts forth in Titanic might, whelming man and the labour of his hands with swiftest, resistless destruction.

At our eventful corner of the earth the proximate cause of the disturbance was the annexation by the Chinese of a newly-discovered and very rich patch of ground called the Green Valley.  Distant some few miles from the actual township, it had been prospected by an old acquaintance of Gus Maynard, an ex-Californian of the wild old days—quite a different sort of person from the orderly and pacific Gus.  Having fallen upon a remarkably rich patch at the head of what he called a 'gulch,' he had marked out his prospecting claim, had come in to report and register—as also to tell a few of his intimate friends, and to 'lay them on,' reserving a certain interest himself.

When he and his friends after a toilsome march returned, Sonora Joe hardly knew the lonely gully among the hills which he had left that morning. They could hear the hum of strange voices, too, long before they reached the place.

'It's them darned Chows,' said Joe wrathfully. 'If I was in hail of Suttor's Mill, and had a few of the old Forty-niners with me, I'd have the ragged bullet through some of their hides before morning. But there's no shooting worth a cent in this cussed country. These blawsted Britishers have no imaginations, darn 'em!'

The scene before him and his mates might have raised a better-tempered man than the scared ex-trapper and Indian fighter. The broad gully was turned into a great Chinese encampment. Lanterns were flitting to and fro, giving a ghoul-like appearance to the strange-costumed, bare-legged figures that moved and chattered in the uncertain light. By the stakes and trenches which Joe's friends tumbled against they could see that hundreds of claims had been marked out, and every inch of the ground legally appropriated. Where did the foreigners all come from ? There were not anything like the number at the Oxley, and what were there were chiefly employed at present on the River Sluicing Claims, about which there had been many quarrels and bitter disputes lately. One boss or headsman had indeed gone so far as to strike his pick into a dam in defiance of the Commissioner before his very face. But the Captain, snatching a revolver from a trooper, had put it to his ear, and dragging him out from among his astonished comrades, handed him over to the sergeant, by whom he was carefully locked up for the night. He was only released upon his payment of a fine of five pounds and a week's imprisonment for disobeying a Commissioner.

' Wal, I heard there was a big camp of these darned skunks, under two bosses, making their way across the mountains,' said Sonora Joe. ' They've had a fresh shipload or two for the Six Companies. But some of them, or this child, 'll have to go under before I lose my ground, if the whole British army was here, and the United States' regulars to help 'em.'

When they went up to the claim which he

had left almost virgin in the morning, Sonora Joe cursed and swore with frightfully elaborate profanity. Beside his very pegs, which had been pulled up, sat a fat and stolid 'Heathen Chinee' whose gratified expression of countenance contrasted strangely with the deadly scowl which darkened the Caucasian features. The claim itself had evidently been rooted about in an unscientific and exasperating manner; while some of the wash-dirt, piled in a heap close by, showed that the Mongolian instinct for gold had not been at fault. Sonora Joe rushed forward and, seizing the astonished pagan by the pigtail, dragged him to his feet, and then hurled him violently to the ground.

'Clear out of this, you infernal yaller image!' roared the infuriated miner, 'pig-rooting a man's very prospecting claim, as if it was "old ground." Hav'n't ye eyes to see pegs and trenches? By all the devils from here to Lone Mountain, I'll have the next man's life that comes inside them pegs agin.'

But the men of a superior race were not likely to have things all their own way on such an occasion. Numbers give boldness even to the most timid animals. The man who had

been thus rudely ejected raised himself with
difficulty and yelled out several words in an unknown tongue.    In an instant the human hive
was aroused—it was not long before it began to
demonstrate the possession of stings.    Sonora
Joe and his mates were bold and hardy men,
not unaccustomed to fight against odds.    They
made for some time a desperate stand.    Fortunately they were not armed with revolvers, as
would have inevitably been the case in their
own land.    But with the long-handled shovels
and other mining tools which lay scattered on
the claim they made a desperate rally, and more
than once drove back the thronging foe.

Still they were powerless after a while against
the forest of sticks which appeared to surround
them, with thickly-flying stones, even more
serious and disabling in their effects.    After a
short but obstinate conflict they were compelled
to beat a retreat; and when they reached the
Oxley about daylight, sore and bruised, wounded
and discomfited, to tell the tale that the whole of
the Green Gully, for which a large division of
their fellow-miners had been preparing to start
that very day, was monopolised by the invading
foreigner, nothing was wanting to supply the

torch for the fires of insurrection which had been smouldering so long.

The day which succeeded this occurrence was long remembered on the Oxley, at Yatala, and indeed throughout the length and breadth of Australia.

Soon after sunrise, both the heralds of the community were observed to patrol the streets with increased solemnity of mien and preternatural importance of visage as they sounded forth, in the intervals of their tintinnabulary warnings, the customary formula for convention of the goldfields *gemote*.

'Roll up, roll up. All true miners are requested to attend a monster meeting at twelve o'clock sharp, opposite the Court-house, to consider the injustice which has been done to the mining community by the Chinese monopoly at Green Gully. Not a yard of this rich alluvial find now available for Europeans. The prospectors ill-used and hunted. Roll up, roll up!'

# CHAPTER XX

NUMBERLESS verbal invitations of this nature
had been heard before at Yatala. At the
Warraluen and other gold towns, time after
time the ominous words 'roll up' had sounded
forth, generally followed up by the gathering of
a mighty crowd to listen eagerly to stormy,
excited oratory. Then the throng would
gradually disperse. A committee would be
formed, with instructions to embody the wrongs
of the mining community in a petition to the
Minister for Lands, who at that period, before
the inauguration of a special department with
a Minister for Mines, swayed their destinies.
Sometimes the wrongs complained of were
imaginary, much fomented by demagogues and
public-house politicians for their own ends.
Sometimes they had real foundation in fact.
In all cases they received recognition, often-

times a measure of redress. This last was occasionally tardy.

The Commissioner and Mr. Merlin were wont to regard these mass meetings, with their fiery denunciations, as convenient safety valves. The sergeant, who knew more of the subterranean igneous agencies, assented in a general way to this doctrine, but thought 'the field' required ceaseless watch and ward in case of accidents. Wide as had been the experience of his superior officers, they had reached the stage of careless confidence, akin to that of the sea-captain who has weathered tempests and grazed a thousand shoals. High-handed and daring to apparent recklessness, how many a threatened goldfield's *émeute*, when battalions of stalwart, strong-willed men had blocked the narrow streets, making the very earth to shake with their tread, had they seen evaporate harmlessly ? It would be so again.

On this morning, however, though all the officials appeared careless and unheeding as usual, they could not conceal from themselves that matters were different. There was something in the air that boded evil. All needful precautions were taken. The small force of police, mounted and on foot, were placed under arms and ready for immediate service. Even a detachment of troopers, passing through to another district, was impressed and added to the contingent ; thus making up an effective army of about thirty men, to assail or defend themselves from thirty thousand ! As rank after rank of miners gathered at the open space in the centre of the town near the camp, as every flat and gully within miles—for scouts had been sent forth from early dawn—furnished forth its quota of volunteers, the crowd became larger, denser, enormous. It was soon openly stated that every claim on the field was idle on that day. Yet there was hardly as much excitement as usual ; no loud talking, no eager gestures. A grave settled resolve—the most dangerous feature of a revolutionary crowd—appeared to have taken possession of the vast assemblage. The open space near the camp—the 'plaza' as the Spanish-American diggers called it—was one sea of human heads. The cross-streets were crowded far down on either side. A rude scaffolding had been erected some time since for the purpose of a hustings on the election of a member for the electorate. Upon this a man suddenly sprang and raised his hand, and as he did so a hoarse cry of greeting, a roar as of a herd of mammoths, rose from the vast far-spreading crowd.   It was one of those sounds which, heard for the first time, instinctively thrill the heart and cause every nerve to vibrate.   It tells of that vast unmanageable force, the physical power of the people, cast loose from all ancient moorings, and drifting into a sea of chaos.   It tells of the unchained lions that are hungry for a prey.   It pronounces, in trumpet-tones, the knell of legitimate authority.   And it thunders the accusation against those whose task it is to guide mankind, that they have been slothful or incapable in the supreme hour of trial.

The man who was thus greeted was dressed in the ordinary garments of a working miner. His flannel shirt was open above his bare breast.   His clay-stained boots and trousers showed that he had been summoned from daily labour.   Yet one could see that he was a man of mark—one of those strange heralds of doom, arising suddenly, like storm-birds which sweep around the lowering horizon over the moaning sea when the tempest's hour is nigh.

As he raised his hand and stepped forward with a free unstudied gesture, and commenced in a resonant vibratory voice, that pierced even to the outer billows of the heaving human sea, Mr. Merlin observed to the Commissioner—

'It's that infernal scoundrel, Radetsky. I thought he was dead. Where has he been hiding all this time?'

'Faith, that's your business,' said the Captain. 'He's worth more than a thousand men where he is this day. After all, he's not a bad fellow that I know of—except that he's a rioter, a democrat *enragé*, and a Pole.'

'He's an infernal firebrand,' growled Merlin, 'and a deserter, I believe. I wish to heavens the Russians had shot him when they caught him, instead of letting him loose to plague us here. The sergeant knows him well.'

'It's me that does,' said that honest officer; 'didn't I know him at Turonia and Rocky Flat, and wasn't he nearly raising a ruction at both places, let alone Ballarat, where they say he was in the stockade. He's a dangerous man, none more so; but he never gave us a chance to run him in.'

'He has got his innings now,' said the Commissioner. 'And what he'll score before he's clean bowled no man can tell.'

The hour had come, and the man. So much was evident. As the burning words of the exile rolled forth in sonorous, telling periods, in spite of his foreign air and accent, the heart of every man in the vast congregation went out to him. He told them how their interests had been systematically sacrificed by those who should have conserved them. How they had been taxed directly and indirectly for the purpose of subsidising a costly system of management, which was as inefficient as expensive. How that their time and their industry had been swallowed up in litigation. How arbitrary rulers had coerced them, threatened them, degraded the very name of free miners, ay, of free manhood. How the whole system of tyranny and misgovernment had culminated in this one last intolerable grievance — this pandering to a monstrous wrong. This handing over the richest portions of the waste country they had civilised, the gold they had discovered, to a pagan horde, ignorant alike of the laws of God and man—human locusts sent hither by the Devil to eat up the reward

of their skilled labour, of their arduous toil,
of their weary exile. He spoke now to the
hearts of men who, like himself, had left
behind them for evermore home and friends
and Fatherland. (Here such a cheer rose
from the foreigners and many of the British
miners as seemed to rend the very air and
echo among the forest glades for long moments
afterwards.) They might suffer this if they
pleased. They might humbly stand and look
on while their comrades were plundered and
their birthright given to dogs. For him, he
was resolved. It was not the first time he
had shed his blood for freedom. He might
rot in gaol. He might die by the sword or
the bullets of hirelings. But, if he tamely
suffered these wrongs, he was no longer a son
of slaughtered, betrayed, buried Poland, and
no longer was his name Stanislas Radetsky.

He stood for one moment as he concluded
his impassioned appeal, in which the words
had poured forth in one unbroken torrent of
sound, emphasised with action that seemed
the very language of his physical being, an
electrical co-ordinate of his nature. Then he
waved his hand with a gesture of defiance as

if to an unseen foe, and leaping lightly down
from the rude rostrum was lost in the crowd.

Then arose, first a hoarse, deep murmur, as
when the ocean slowly thunders against the
rock-battlements ere the storm-wind arises in
its might, bearing on its breath, in rudely
rhythmical monotone, the doom of lonely
barques, of strong-sailed navies and their
crews.   Then came a storm of cheers, commenced near the place where the speaker had
subsided, and taken up from time to time till
the furthermost edge of the vast concourse
of people was reached.   From time to time
the menacing sound-waves ceased—only to be
taken up and renewed at the slightest outburst.

'What do you think of that, Merlin?' said
the Commissioner.

'By —— ! they mean mischief at last,'
replied that official.   'I was always doubtful
that those infernal Chinamen would lead to a
row some day.   I wish I'd telegraphed for a
double supply of men.'

'Not the least use, my dear fellow,' said the
Commissioner.   'If these fellows are as far gone
as you say a company of regulars would make
no earthly difference.'

'That's impossible to say—and, surely, I
need not explain to Captain Blake,' replied
Merlin, with his most superfine bow, 'what a
very small proportion of disciplined troops is
sufficient to awe a crowd, however numerous.'

'There are crowds and crowds, my dear
fellow,' answered the Commissioner, patting
one of his greyhounds, who looked wistfully
at the great array, divining with the instinct
of his race that things were not as usual.
'Ban here knows that there's no kangarooing
for him to-day, and he does not offer to run
in any of the people as he generally does on
Saturdays. Who is getting up now? No
foreigner this time, eh?'

'It's Mark Thursby. I wonder at his
making a fool of himself; but they're all going
mad together, it seems to me.'

'By Jove! so it is. My favourite digger,
if I have a preference for one of them. Serves
me right; but it looks bad when old Mark
Thursby begins to "revolute."'

A very different figure from the eager,
impassioned Pole now slowly arose and raised
himself to his full height. A broad, vast-
chested, long-armed figure, roughly clad, with

heavy hob-nailed boots neatly laced up to
the ankle.   One of those children of labour
whom the kindly soil and temperate clime of
Britain have reared to till the fields, to work
her thousand-fathom-deep mines, to build her
endless iron roads, to be a marvel and a boast for
strength and manliness the wide world through.

An Englishman he, and born north of the
Humber ; so much was evident from his speech
the moment he opened his mouth.   That he
was a representative man and popular with
his fellows was also demonstrated by the
cheers and favourable cries which greeted his
appearance.

Standing erect and looking calmly at the
vast surging mass, he spoke without a hint,
gesture, or outward sign.   His deep voice was
but little raised, still it could be heard by those
at a considerable distance away, so complete
and wonderful was the hush.   This was a
proved doer, not a talker ; a man of immense
personal weight and influence.   And his every
shred of utterance was valued according to its
rarity.   An untiring worker, yet a man of
great organising power in mining under-
takings.   Utterly honest, fearless, true, and

steadfast, there was not a boy on the whole of the Oxley diggings, out to the most distant unimportant gully, where a few ounces of gold were gathered weekly, who did not know, had not heard of Mark Thursby of Eaglehawk.

'I'm for the law mostly, you all know,' he said. 'Noan ivir seed me along o' the Coort, or in t' Logs ; and I've been diggin' since '49 at Suttor's Mill. But things has gotten too bad, though aw've nowt to say agin the Commissioner nor Mr. Merlin nor agin the sargint, as is a reet doon sensible chap as ever put the darbies on a Christian mon. But summat's gan clean wrong, and that bad as needs ravellin' oot, where yaller Chayneymen is gotten that bold as they'll tak' t' brass and the land both, and drive out diggers as has paid for their Rights, and Englishmen as do'ant reckon to knock under to any folk on God's earth whatever colour or talk they've gotten. And if you're all good for gannin' reet oot to Green Gully and takkin' it back from 'em, Mark Thursby's for makkin' one.'

The hoarse roar which greeted this proposition, unadorned as was the bare statement of fact with any flowers of rhetoric, was sufficient to denote that the deeper passions of the multitude were stirred. Those who listened were fully aware that something unusual was imminent. Of the nature and full extent they could hardly judge. Another and yet another speaker sprang forward and addressed the crowd, both representative miners, and men who had shared the experiences, the toils, and the burdens of those whom they addressed. Still no further manifestations of feeling took place. The great mass gradually became disintegrated, and the miners in small knots and companies departed. But it was known in the camp that the word had been passed round for a full muster at daybreak. What the result of that gathering might be all might surmise, but none could with certainty divine.

A sort of council of war was held, at which the sergeant, with Mr. Merlin and the Commissioner, assisted.

The sergeant looked so grave that the Commissioner, who had a strong dash of reckless hardihood about him, commenced to laugh.

'It's no laughing matter, Blake,' said Mr. Merlin. 'In my opinion the barricades are morally up, and to-morrow's sun will rise on the largest goldfield in Australia in revolt.'

'Against which we have a force?' queried
the Commissioner.

'Of thirty strong, including all branches of
the service,' said Merlin, with a mock solemnity ;
'cavalry, infantry, with a reserve of two lock-up
keepers.'

'Well, we must conquer or die, it seems,'
said Captain Blake carelessly. 'I sha'n't retreat
if there were forty thousand instead of thirty.
I don't suppose they will thirst for our blood,
however indignant they may be with regulations
that don't exclude Chinamen. We must tem-
porise as well as we can until the Government
sends reinforcements, which they are quite
certain to do within a week.'

.     .     .     .     .     .

While this movement was going on, it may
be imagined that our party felt personally
interested after no trifling fashion. We had
everything to lose and nothing to gain by conflict with the civil power. Any overturning of
the present state of society might be ruinous to
us socially and financially. If we got mixed up
with the rioters, we might be joined in their
future defeat and punishment. If a general
scramble took place, we might lose our claim.

We had no fancy for being ruled over by the truculent scoundrels, of whom there were numbers among the mining body, only kept down by pressure of law and the orderly feeling of the masses. Our opinions were shared by large numbers of the better educated miners. Nevertheless, so strong was the *esprit de corps* which had grown up through years of mining comradeship, so fixed and clear was the conviction that in the matter of the Chinese our order had suffered wrong, that we felt bound in honour, and indeed irresistibly impelled to identify ourselves with the movement, disastrous though it might be to all our best interests. At the same time, we were not without hope that we might exercise a beneficial influence upon the crowd, thus possibly preventing bloodshed or overt acts of rebellion.

When, therefore, we were visited by the committee formed for the purpose of organising resistance to this present legalised Chinese occupation, we gave in our adhesion, only expressing our hope that order would be maintained, and that nothing more would be done than was necessary to assert constitutional rights.

'You bet we're not going to let the rowdies have it their own way any more than the Chows,' said Sonora Joe, who was one of the selected chiefs of our auriferous republic. 'If any of them begin to show out and out ugly, we'll teach 'em what the Associated Miners' Executive Committee can do. There's some of 'em that remember San Francisco, and the old Vigilante days too well to make much of a muss. And, Major, I'm deputed to ask you, sir, in the name of the miners of the Oxley, now engaged in this little *pronunciamiento*, if you'll act as chief magistrate and commissioner in any cases that may be brought before you. We're bound to administer justice while we're working out the Magna Charta business; and I reckon Captain Blake won't feel free to act till things is fixed up square and monarchical again.'

'I don't expect he will,' said the Major, smiling rather grimly. 'And for two pins I wouldn't either. But just to keep things straight, I'll take office with you Roundheads temporarily. But remember, if it comes to resisting the Queen's troops, I'm against you to the last drop of my blood.'

'We don't expect nothin' else, Major,' said

the Republican. 'We don't expect any Queen's officer to desert his colours—we must all fend for ourselves then. Mayhap it won't come to that. But they must give us up the ground as we've toiled and moiled and wasted our lives for, or there'll be more than one as 'll stand a shot for it. Daylight's the word and Green Gully.'

This important colloquy took place about midnight after the monster meeting in the town. All the early part of the night preparations were made, sub-committees were formed, each having power to act in certain contingencies. The miners have the faculty of organisation to a considerable extent, and for the necessity of self-government which has arisen under many circumstances of their migrating lives, are by no means so much at sea as large bodies of men suddenly cut loose from the social fabric would be apt to be. Soon after midnight, therefore, all arrangements had been made, and the goldfield was in repose, which gave an utterly false impression of the state of tranquillity and the subsistence of lawless intent.

But long before the stars had left the sky the whole encampment was astir; and as the

sun rose, the measured tread of ten thousand
men marching towards the police camp commenced to shake the earth, and to warn the
occupants with that strange indescribable hum
which a large approaching force, however
silently disposed, always produces, that the
miners of the Oxley were at length under
arms.

# CHAPTER XXI

A STRICT watch had been kept at the camp the whole night through. In the ghostly dawn, gray creeping o'er darksome hill and hollow, the figures could be faintly discerned of armed men who, with their centurion, stood at their posts, as did the Roman sentinels in long-buried cities before the gloom and crash of the volcano. Yet, as the van of the great hosts of insurgents neared them, the wings of which stretched as far as could be seen, some natural anxiety must have arisen as to their intentions in approaching the tiny citadel. The police barracks and temporary gaol, popularly termed 'the Logs,' from the massive timber employed in all parts of their construction, were substantial if rude edifices, calculated to stand a siege against any reasonably superior attacking force. But the present league, if such it proved to be, would

be as the tidal-wave of the ocean to the fisher-
man's boat-shed—the lake-flood to the beaver-
dam.   A few shots might be fired in desperation;
a score or two of the rioters killed and wounded.
And then every man in uniform would lose his
life, had he a dozen to spare—might even be
lynched or torn limb from limb by the infuriated
rioters.   Crowds, in their delirious hour, have
been cruel ere now.

Still no sign of unsteadiness should be shown
by the representatives of law.   The officers
were grave and resolved; the men firm, in
their usual mechanical state of non-inquiring
obedience.

'There are enough of them to eat us,' said
Captain Blake.   'I wonder what the beggars
are going to do?   That's Radetsky in front
carrying the flag.   But they're not all such
crack-brained enthusiasts as he is.   Sonora
Joe is near him, and our friends, the Major,
Harry Pole, and that big Cornstalk.   They
will all be for moderation.   I see some other
fellows I don't like so well; but we must take
our chance.   Here they come.'

The leading body, having made a short
wheel, now advanced to the edge of the open

space in front of the police camp. I most un-
willingly displayed myself in semi-martial array.
All who possessed them carried revolvers.
Radetsky had girded on an old cavalry sword.

'We must go out and meet them,' I heard
Mr. Merlin say distinctly. 'Hang it, we'll show
them we're not afraid. Attention! left wheel!
march!'

The police troopers and foot constables, who
are always instructed in infantry drill at an early
stage of their career, immediately stepped out
after the immovable British fashion, making as if
they were about to advance in the very teeth of
the aroused multitude. Merlin himself, on his
gray Arab, rode on at their head as though he
had the command of something like an equal
force. We could hear him say, 'Steady, men,
mark time!' as the little band executed their
manœuvre with most creditable precision.

The Commissioner, with his usual expression
of half-humorous gravity, loungingly sat on his
well-known horse, close to whose feet his greyhounds crowded, looking wistfully at the multitude as if, with the fine instinct of their species,
they had divined that a storm was imminent.

So invariably accustomed were the greater

portion of the people to render implicit submission to the law as represented by the personages
now present, that even when their absurd
inadequacy as combatants was so sharply contrasted, a curious feeling of schoolboy shame-
facedness and moral inferiority was uppermost
for the moment.   Then the reactionary element
prevailed, and with a mingled sentiment of
admiration for the dauntless front of the small
army of regulars and a half-painful derision of
their own instinctive deference, a storm of cheers
burst from the multitude, which was taken up
again and again, till the forest rang to its mountain buttresses.

The Commissioner promptly seized the opportunity, and in a sonorous, resolute voice
addressed them.

'Sorry to see you here, men, in open defiance
of the law, threatening the Queen's representatives.   I do not deny your grievances, but by
constitutional means, and those only, they would
have been redressed.   Now, at the bidding of
bad advisers, you have deliberately chosen to
use physical force, thereby placing yourselves
in the false position of rebels and outlaws
against the Queen's Government.'

(Here there was a hoarse ominous murmur, with cries of—'We'll show the Sydney officials we're not to be trampled on.')

'You know I don't mince my words, and always speak my mind to you. I shall do so now. Take my advice and go back to your work. Represent your cause of complaint, which I will see duly brought before the Government, and will back up with all the means in my power, for in the Chinese question I am quite of your way of thinking. (Cheers.) But, once commit yourselves to lawless acts and you'll all repent it. Mr. Merlin, here, and myself, can do nothing with our handful of men, good as they are. We cannot rout twenty thousand men or take them prisoners. So we shall not try. But, mark my words—that you will have every man of the 70th Regiment, down to the drummer boys, up here within a month, the volunteers and all sailors and marines that may be on the station. Can't you see that you *must* be beaten if they bring artillery with them—perhaps some of you shot or hanged, who knows? You have not gone too far as yet, though your attitude is disorderly. Take my advice — don't be led away by foreigners, and trust to your own

Government and your own officers.    They have always dealt out justice, and will again.'

Here Mr. Bagstock, who had been an unwilling participator in the inconveniences of the bivouac, anticipating even yet more undesirable experiences, impatiently broke in, shouting to supplement practically and effectively his superior officer's speech.

'Look here, m-m-men,' he said; 'w-w-what's the use of all this m-m-mummery? it's b-b-beastly cold, this w-w-watching, I can t-t-tell you! Suppose you go and r-r-r-register block claims in G-g-green Gully—most of those Ch-ch-chows haven't got Miners' Rights, you know—that's the easiest way to g-g-get possession, and quite l-l-legal too.'

A tremendous burst of laughter followed this proposition, made with the greatest coolness and apparent earnestness, joined with cries of—

'Well done you, Mr. Bagstock, you stay and stick to your papers.    We won't touch a hair of your head,' etc.

The point of the joke, however, which was that Mr. Bagstock received a fee for each act of registration, and that in this hour of danger he had been sufficiently wide awake to his own

interests to suggest the registration of a revolutionary mob at half-a-crown a head, so tickled
the more humorous spirits that their infectious
mirth went far to divert the rioters from their
stern purposes. Even the iron-visaged police
troopers could scarcely control their features,
albeit under the terrible eye of Mr. Merlin.

The sergeant stared fiercely at an adjacent
gum-tree, while the Commissioner slapped Mr.
Bagstock jocularly on the back, and declared he
would rise in the Civil Service, to which he was
an honour and an ornament.

This ludicrous *contretemps*, joined with the
sensible address of the Commissioner, whom all
respected and believed, nearly had the effect of
allaying irritation and sending most of the men
back to their homes. But exorcists of all lands,
since the world's dimmest eld, have ever found
the fiend more easy to invoke than to lay. So
it was in the present state of matters. All the
worst characters in the various mining camps
were now gathered together. Also, those mer-
curial spirits upon whom numbers and opportunity act as a spell for evil, found their fitting
sphere and opportunity. The moderate men
were overpowered by the subtle influence of an

aroused multitude, while the wilder elements rejoiced recklessly in their hour of triumph. Scarcely had the legitimate miners raised their voices to cheer the Commissioner, and to suggest that after all they had better leave the matter in his hands, than a storm of cries, howls, and a surging rush towards the camp showed that the time of temporising measures was past.

'What!' shouted the fierce exile, maddened by the fear of losing his last chance of revolt against a settled government, and mingling in his excited brain a host of old-world wrongs with present grievances, 'are we to go back like beaten hounds at the beck of a tyrant, an oppressor of the people, who looks upon the toiling masses as dogs, the minion of a despotic Government, based as are all Governments upon the blood and labour of the foolish people, of us—of us! whom they chain and enslave and rob, and flog and slay—do I not, Stanislas Radetsky, bear the marks of their accursed rods? And are we to be lower than Chinese? But I will strike the first blow for liberty, let who will follow! Comrades, advance, we must have the camp!'

As he spoke he rushed towards the police,
his eyes glaring with half-maniacal fury, and
fired his pistol point-blank at Mr. Merlin, who
sat unmoved upon his well-drilled horse, as one
hardly believing that any actual overt act of
warfare would follow. At the same time a few
dropping shots were fired by men evidently
acting in concert with Radetsky, who no doubt
had been secretly working for a more com-
pendious scheme of revolt.

The sudden report seemed to transform the
impassive Merlin, who promptly gave the word
—fire! and at the same time, raising his revolver
without any appearance of haste, fired at the
self-constituted leader, who staggered, but was
immediately lifted up by those nearest to him
and carried inward. At the same time an
effective volley was fired by the whole body of
police, who then retreated in good order towards
their camp. I heard a bullet or two whiz
unpleasantly near me. I saw the man on my
left throw up his arms and drop in a ghastly
heap by my side. And I was then hurried
forward as by a resistless wave by the maddened
crowd, which passed onward with overwhelming
force.

Then, indeed, ensued a tumult such as no man could imagine or describe, and such as in all my previous experience I had never dreamed of. Cries and curses, groans and shrieks, as an occasional bullet sped home, arose from all around. In vain did those in the van try to stem the mad rush onward, not willing to mix themselves up with the insane act of Radetsky, and unwilling to provoke a further firing from the police, who had only given a second volley, and stopped as soon as the fire from our side ceased. All order was lost. All feeling merged, apparently, in mad demoniac rage and thirst for blood and vengeance.

The police had retreated within their citadel, which was capable of being well and effectively defended, as long as their ammunition should hold out. Built with a view to resist a sudden onslaught, it was massively constructed of heavy hard-wood logs. The heavy doors were strong and clamped with iron. It was not particularly easy to set on fire, so that deadliest of all resorts of the besieger was in abeyance. The iron-bark shingles defied hasty ignition, so that the besieged with their repeating rifles could have shot down any number of men engaged in

carrying combustibles.  Moreover, the timber
cleared away by the reckless use of firewood by
a large population left bare considerable space
around the camp.   Hence, even with the immensely superior attacking force, it was seen
that they had a long and dangerous task before
them in compelling the surrender of the little
fortress.   To storm it would have been a
most useless expenditure of blood, and only
justifiable in the case of the death of every
single one of the garrison being resolved upon.
Such few shots as had been fired by the police
had been more deterrent than irrevocably
disastrous fortunately.   Radetsky was badly
but apparently not mortally wounded.   Others
were more or less hurt, but no man had been
slain outright.   The rioters, much worked upon
by all the moderate party, among whom Mark
Thursby, the Major, the Bulders, and myself
of course, canvassed unremittingly, began to
consider whether it was worth while sitting
down for a lengthened siege before the un-
promising-looking camp, where the police could
certainly hold out for several days, or whether
they had better go on and drive out the Chinese,
who after all were legitimate enemies, in pos-

session of their gold and the cause of the whole disturbance.

Here Sonora Joe, who meant business rather than revolt, and who was extremely cute, like most of his countrymen, in the management of the sovereign people, saw his way to a diversion.

'I don't see,' he commenced, as soon as the turmoil had sufficiently subsided to secure him a hearing, 'what all this army work is going to do with getting back our shallow ground in Green Gully! Here's these cussed Chows working away and rootin' out the gold like spuds, while we're foolin' round these darned old logs and waitin' for the myrmidons of this all-fired, old Sydney one-horse Government to shoot some more of us. They can't well be off it—and when we've got all these boys' scalps in the block-house, I don't see how we can realise on 'em. They won't be half as good trade as those shallow claims, and we're losing them all the time. Guess we'd better make tracks ; put the prospectors back on to their claims ; wire in on the block, and send the hull darned lot o' those yaller niggers to h—l.'

This characteristic address, more particularly

the concluding sentiment, seemed at this
juncture to strike the fancy of the capricious
crowd mightily. The artful allusion to rich
gold in shallow workings, the miners' Eldorado,
was difficult to resist. Nothing but hard
knocks were to be got by staying where they
were. Gold, adventure, revenge, were to be
obtained by the onward march. Our party
enthusiastically applauded and indeed took the
lead for Green Gully, whither we had the
satisfaction to find ourselves followed by the
whole crowd, a comparatively small force being
left to guard the guardians of the peace.

It may have been some seven or eight miles
from the Oxley proper to the Green Gully.
A concourse of individuals, whether brute or
human, does not advance so quickly as a smaller
number. Nevertheless, once started on the
road every man apparently put his best leg
forward, and very good time was made. Was
it not a 'rush'? That magic word in mining
parlance! How many times had we all seen
people strip themselves of the last shilling, the
last shred of property they had in the world, to
improve their fortune by risking their lives to
ensure their chances of being early at a rush

which was perhaps utterly worthless and barren when they got there.

For the miner proper, splendid possibilities seem to be the resistless lure, and he is so constituted that the undefined mysterious future is quite sufficient to overbalance the prosaic present, however satisfactory and solvent soever.

In this case the majority had made up their minds that Green Gully combined the profits of a 'rush' with the excitement of a revolt, and their gamblers' nature was stirred accordingly to its lowest depths.

After little more than two hours' march we came in sight of the far-famed Green Gully, the fame of which was soon to be so widely bruited abroad. There we saw a horde of yellow men, the Huns of this gold-empire of ours, spread over it apparently with the multiform ceaseless industry of an ant-hill.

A hoarse roar broke from the crowd as they marked the steady passage of lines of workers from the claim to the creek, bearing on their shoulders what they knew to be rich wash-dirt, —or why should they so sedulously keep up the laborious process of washing and 'cradling' the ore?

'There's my prospecting claim as thick as a
bit of honeycomb with ants, blast 'em!' cried
out Sonora Joe.   'Isn't that enough to make a
white man own himself first cousin to a blind
mule in a sugar-mill?   Is this what we came
across those infernal sage brush deserts to
'Frisco, and across sea hyar fur?   Is the British
Empire played out? and is this here Miner's
Right a bit of waste paper?'

Then he drew out the parchment document
so well known to his hearers, and flourished it
on high, as though it had been the title-deed of
the whole Caucasian race.

The effect was electrical.   By this time the
main army of miners, with camp-followers and
concomitant personages of all kinds, had arrived,
and were, so to speak, broadside on to the
incurious automatons of Celestials, who went
on without sign of doubt or trepidation, yarning
up the yellow dross as though their privilege
was to last to the day of doom.   Such was it,
in fact, to them.

With a hungry sudden rush as of one man,
the vast crowd, like a tidal wave, rolled on and
over the host of inferior race.   It was an
instant mean eclipse, followed by annihilation.

The next moment, as it seemed, the whole
superficial area of the Green Gully was occupied
with European miners.   In every direction were
seen Chinese flying madly in panic, their pigtails floating behind them, their loose clothes
fluttering in the breeze, their slippers discarded
or only visible on one foot, their broad-brimmed
hats flying in the breeze or lying prone and
curiously suggestive on the earth.   Picks and
shovels were raised in the *mêlée*, not altogether
in vain.   The Chinese that remained were
kicked, struck down, hustled, in every way
maltreated until they joined, like the rest, the
unreasoning panic of which they had been the
victims.   Sonora Joe, waving a brace of pigtails suspiciously resembling scalps at the thicker
ends, bore down on the dignified and supercili-
ous boss, who had so quietly sat down upon his
prospecting claim.   He was then running and
yelling in the most ignominious manner.   Joe
could not avoid the triumph of sounding a war-
whoop over his departure, and intensifying by
a simple stratagem his agony and despair at
the onslaught of the white barbarians.

   In half an hour all was apparently quiet.
Sonora Joe was again in possession of his

prospecting claim. Many of the others had
apparently taken up claims with the greatest
promptitude and despatch. There was not a
bit of spare ground left in the whole Green
Gully. A couple of thousand men were settled,
apparently, upon as rich a bit of alluvial as had
been seen or heard of since old Eaglehawk.
The great thing was to keep it.

'Fancy a mob of Chinamen getting hold of
a bit of ground like this,' said more than one
steady-going old hand, delighted to quit the
conflict for easy sinking. 'Let's see who'll
turn us out again.'

As for the constables at the camp, they had
nearly forgotten all about them. They could
forgive them, and only trusted they wouldn't
make fools of themselves and bring more bloodshed and danger on their heads.

In those days the area of the claims was
small, so that, as the combatants carefully re-
tained the legal measurement as between one
another, the Green Gully, which was patently
rich, absorbed a very large proportion of the
leading miners, and also of the dangerous
classes. In a comparatively short time the
rapid transformation, therefore, had taken place

from an invading army into a body of peaceful miners wielding pick and shovel, or marking out their claims with painstaking accuracy. Of the routed Celestials not a solitary individual remained. After à hurried consultation they had formed themselves into some kind of marching order, and departed at a jog-trot in the direction whence they had come.

# CHAPTER XXII

FOR ourselves, we took no part in the attack and ill-treatment of the aliens. Of course we held such to be unlawful and indefensible, though from a miner's point of view we could easily understand an excited mob of mixed nationalities acting in that way. We had abstained from all complicity in the violence done, and took no share in the reward. We doubted not but that some kind of expiation was likely to be exacted for these high-handed proceedings, and were resolved to keep as clear of all blame as our comrades would permit us to do.

We, therefore, took the earliest opportunity of going back to the Oxley, though we had some difficulty in persuading Cyrus Yorke not to 'wire in,' as he expressed it, for 'a bit of shaller, with the gold sticking out a-beggin', for half an hour, with a Chinaman's pick and shovel, cradle and everything complete.' We dwelt upon the anxiety such a proceeding would cause his wife, and finally carried him safely back with us.

On our arrival at the camp we discovered, to our great gratification, that the whole body of officials, with the police, had executed a flank movement and retired in good order, having evacuated their fortress and fallen back upon reinforcements. The force which had been left to keep them in check had found the task irksome, and gradually melted away. A scout had come in from Green Gully and given such glowing accounts of the extraordinary richness and shallowness of the ground—the best thing seen by living men since Eaglehawk in Victoria —that it was not in the nature of miners to stay away from such a rush. All the more energetic took their departure incontinently, leaving behind a gradually decreasing band of earnest political enthusiasts, with a sprinkling of loafers and camp-followers.

When these, towards nightfall, saw the Commissioner, followed by Mr. Merlin and his men, come forth in battle array, and take the road to

Warraluen, they did not see their way clear to withstand them, and evidently thought, like that Provost of Edinburgh who considered the good town 'weel rid of that deil of Dundee,' that it was well to connive at the retreat of such unpleasant, possibly dangerous adversaries.

On the following morning, therefore, when a contingent from the main body of the rioters, having had leisure to return temporarily from their claims and devote a little time to public affairs, discovered that the camp was empty, they took formal possession of the silent cells and echoing court-house and offices in the name of the Committee of Public Safety and the Associated Miners of Australia.

It was now certain that the bolder spirits among them entertained a hope that this revolt would spread through the whole mining population of New South Wales, at that time numerically large and powerful, and that the working classes *en masse* would next follow suit. To this end, and to fit themselves for future republican responsibilities, they commenced to make laws for their own guidance, and to administer the present code in a temper which showed that they would not permit anarchy, violence, or petty crime among their own body.

Thus a few low-lived ruffians, who had presumed on the social dislocation to pilfer and threaten outrage, were at once arrested and lodged in the cells, being locked up with as much promptitude as in the day of the sergeant's rule.

On the next morning they were tried before an elected committee of miners and sentenced to a week's solitary confinement on bread and water, with a significant hint that on the second offence the more severe Californian penalties would be inflicted. This had the desired effect. An example was at once shown and terror struck into those baser natures that can be ruled in no other way. We and others who had valuable claims were not sorry to see that order would be enforced. We, therefore, in every way assisted by personal influence and otherwise to sustain so desirable a state of self-government.

That the bank officials did not by any means approve of the present state of matters may be supposed. They saw themselves surrounded by a heterogeneous population from whom the

ordinary restraints had been suddenly withdrawn.   At any moment an organised band of
desperadoes might arrange to make a descent
upon any given bank when it was well known
that thousands of pounds' worth of notes and
sovereigns, besides large deposits of gold, were
in their safes.   In a general way these officials
were highly popular; such being the rule
among managers detailed for goldfields work,
and the ordinary mode of life being favourable
to a frank bearing joined with business habi-
tudes.   But they had formerly had all the police
at their backs; the strong arm of the law could
always be invoked for their protection.   Now
they were virtually helpless, merely trusting to
the good faith and honourable feeling of a body
of men who had openly defied the recognised
authorities.   The position was not reassuring.

Superficial readers of the great book of
human nature might have deemed that it was a
favourable time for the return of the bushrangers,
who, since the police had been withdrawn, had
no disciplined force to oppose.   A fatal error!
Had Frank Lardner's gang presumed upon any
feeling of sympathy among the miners their
career would have had a premature ending.

The mining community of the Oxley had
revolted against their rulers and the Government of the day because they saw the hard-won
privileges of their order handed over to an
inferior race, while their remonstrances were
neglected or contemned.    They had openly
stated their grievances, and, failing adequate
redress, had then taken arms against the authorities, in the light of day.    But Lardner, Wall,
and the rest of the gang had proved themselves
assassins in the first instance, and robbers
afterwards.    They had stolen the gold which
represented months of toil, often persevered in
(for the diseases of camps claimed a daily toll)
while the hand was heavy and the heart faint
with sickness nigh unto death.    And had they
shown their faces on the Oxley at that critical
period, Judge Lynch would have been assuredly
presented with a commission, when a quick
trial and a short shrift would very probably
have stamped out robbery under arms, and
saved the lives of scores of better men in the
days that were to come.

No such sensational visitors, however, turned
up.    Even Malgrade, Big Harry, and a few
others of the leading spirits of the Alsatia at

Murderers' Flat, appeared somewhat subdued, having received warning, we afterwards heard, that a corps akin to the Californian Vigilantes was in process of formation.

The committee plainly made it apparent that no irregularity would be tolerated by the mining commune so suddenly organised, excepting that of disestablishing John Chinaman. Gold was plentiful in a general way. The Oxley was what is called 'a good poor man's diggings.' That is, most men—even those who were not lucky—were getting what they called ' wages and a trifle over '—meaning four or five pounds a week. A certain amount of ready money, arising from fairly remunerated labour, equally distributed among the populace, has always— and I speak from experience—an effect conducive to propriety and self-respect. Thus at the Oxley, though it came to my knowledge that a ' big thing ' was planned and very nearly came off, no unlawful interference with the banking treasuries occurred in any one instance during the rule of the provisional government. Indeed, a kind of Utopian order and good guidance for a while prevailed — that kind of government ' of the people for the people by

the people ' for which so many ardent patriots
have written and spoken, have fought and bled,
died by sword and spear, axe and scaffold—
from the dim darksome eld till now. How long
this state of things might have lasted is another
matter.

But it could not be denied by the worst
enemies of democracy that, the *casus belli*
effectually removed, nothing could have been
more satisfactory to a philanthropist than the
appearance and internal condition of the Oxley.
In the streets of our strange city were seen
none of the mournful degraded forms of poverty,
no travesties of human nature, patiently carrying
out a sentence of want, hunger, and degradation
during their stay on earth. There were no poor
in rags, no houseless women, no aged paupers,
no gutter children, no street boys, no outcasts.
All the viler types of humanity which deform
great cities, and even the denser rural populations of the old world, were conspicuous by
their absence. The schools were well and
regularly attended. The churches of the various
denominations, the pastors of which all remained
at their posts, were crowded on the Sabbath.
These good men had in truth never ceased to

exhort to submission and to warn their con-
gregations to keep from all riotous and violent
proceedings.    In a general way they possessed
much influence.    But this was one of the slow
culminating crises—outbursts of human society
—which kings, priests, or rulers are alike
powerless to prevent.

I by no means wish to assert that our
confederated community was free from the
ordinary sins and breaches of the moral law
under this provisional government.    But there
was, as under the old *régime*, a wondrously small
amount of open or shameless evil.    There was
but little perceptible wrong-doing, nothing overt
which would cause the lover of his kind to
grieve and point to the bad influence of the
*auri sacra fames*.    Quite the contrary, in fact.
Whether under our old-world despotism, or the
newer lights of poor Radetsky, Mark Thursby,
and the rest, a more serious, well-mannered,
orderly-appearing settlement than that of the
Oxley did not exist upon the earth.    There
were human beasts of prey among them, doubtless.    They were but as the wolves and pumas
which prowl around a herd of buffaloes.    An
isolated or heedless individual separated from

its fellows might be occasionally beset; but on
the least alarm there are a thousand trampling
feet, a thousand glaring eyes and levelled
horns, ready to crush to earth or toss lifeless
in the air the base intruder, cowardly as
savage.

Even those that were physically unable to
endure the strain of manual labour found here
rest and ease.  A perennial side-stream of
charity, flowing from the main channel of
golden gain, enriched these weaklings and
feeble brethren.  Miners are always free-
handed, so long as the tide of Pactolus runs
not low, and in the patronage of the smaller
industries, or in more direct alms-giving, the
old, the worn-out, and the afflicted found ready
sympathy and ample aid.

One of those invaluable literary caterers for
modern civilisation, ever ready to construct
historiettes concerning lands which he has
never seen and societies which he can never
have entered, describes in one Australian novel
(save the mark) a lovely and distressed damsel,
reft from her friends, and chained to the pole of
a tent by a ruffian band of diggers.  In another
improving tale the prepossessing, if not, perhaps,

immaculate heroine is publicly disposed of by
lottery and carried off by the winner. How
utterly, childishly impossible such occurrences
could have been in the wildest days of mining
adventure, let any digger say. Shades of the
Sergeant! fancy his majestic indignation when,
from information received, he started forth to
arrest such flagrant and foolhardy criminals.

His strides would have lengthened to those
which were conferred upon the wearer of the
seven-leagued boots; his very gaze would have
burned up the perpetrators of so unmanly, so
unparalleled an outrage; and the shortest possible interval would have elapsed between the
first whisper of the atrocities and the safe
lodgment of all the parties to the disgrace
in the historic Logs, *en route* for the district
gaol.

No! that strange scenes have been enacted
in all mining communities I am not pledged to
deny, but as far as my experiences of the Oxley
and Yatala go, premier goldfields of Australia,
on each of which twenty or thirty tons of gold
had been unearthed within five years, where
four millions sterling were divided among thirty
or forty thousand men, such occurrences were not

only never heard of, but were far more impossible
of occurrence than in the very heart of London
or Paris.    Whatever the miners' shortcomings,
the lack of a chivalric courtesy, of a deeply-
rooted respect for womanhood, is not among
them.

Mr. Bright, the manager of the Bank of
New Holland, was so far from being uneasy at
the situation that he positively gloried in the
warlike aspect and 'besieged resident' sort of
business in which we existed.    We all believed
that he would have rather liked the bank to
have been 'stuck up' with fair notice.    A
proverbially good shot and quick with his
weapons, he carried a regular battery about
with him for fear of being suddenly beset.
We used to say that his customers were afraid
to put their hands in their pockets to extricate
a check for fear he might suspect them of
feeling for a revolver and let fly at once.    One
day the Major and I, strolling down the street,
heard a shot in the bank.

'Hallo! Bright has enticed in a band of
robbers at last,' said the Major.    'It's a pity to
spoil his pleasure, but we may as well look in
for fear of accidents.'

When we got in it was another matter
altogether.    Our friend did not look so radiant
and rubicund as usual.    A fume of gunpowder
and a hole in the floor suggested an accidental
shot.    It appeared that he sat down rather
suddenly, and jarring one of the pistols which
he wore round his waist, like the pirate captains
of our youth, a six-shooter exploded, tearing
through his coat-tail and burying a bullet in the
floor unpleasantly near to his big toe.

Congratulations and libations having succeeded, he bewailed his lot in being cast in so
fearful a region.    Not even during a rebellion
had any one the pluck to do anything out of
the common.    However, he had advices that
military and even naval reinforcements were
on the road.    The rebels would be routed and
discomfited in no time.

'How's Radetsky getting on ?    Poor devil!
I shouldn't wonder, Major, when the regulars
come up if they hang all the leaders, yourself
included, on that big tree in the camp reserve.'

'Radetsky will escape their clutches,' the
Major said calmly.    'By Jove! I sometimes
wish I was as near the end as he is.'

'Pooh,    pooh!'    said    the    banker    good-

humouredly, 'wait till that No. 4 of yours is
in full work again, and even without that small
property you can clear out for Europe and pick
up your old form again.    I wish I had the
chance.'

'Something always seems to come in the
way of our luck,' said the Major.    'First,
those scoundrels of jumpers, and then this
beastly *émeute* about Chinamen.   I suppose we
shall have a Russian invasion next, if the claim
is proved good in law.'

On the following day it was announced that
Radetsky was dying.    The fiery enthusiast, the
excited patriot, the descendant of an ancient
line and representative of a gallant nation, was
about to end his days in a rude hut in a mining
settlement in a far, half-unknown land.    He
whose childhood had been passed among nobles
and princes, petted by fond relatives, ministered
to by devoted servants, was now dying alone
and untended save by the charitable offices of
his 'mate,' a peasant compatriot, and the neighbours, as even on a diggings the adjoining
workers are called.

Not that much was wanting which could be
of real benefit to the wounded man.    The hut

was small but scrupulously clean, and no care or watching was omitted that skill or kindness could devise. The principal medical man of the district, a duly qualified surgeon of high attainments and world-wide experience, had attended him from the day of his hurt. It was thought at first that he would recover, as the bullet had not touched any vital portion of his frame. But the man's tameless excitable nature was against him. He could not be induced to keep quiet during the first days of the campaign, and at length, when fever and delirium set in, and the sick man commenced to rave about the Austrian Cuirassiers and the charges against the Imperial troops he had led, to count up his wounds, and to name the name of Haynau with tireless execration, Dr. Burnside told his mate that his time was come.

'He will never make another speech, poor fellow,' said the kind-hearted medico; 'if he had been an Englishman or a German I could have pulled him through, but these Sclaves are as bad as Celts, they *will* subordinate their reason to their emotions. You might as well try to cure an untrained Norway falcon.'

So a few days before the important news of

the arrival of the military put all other matters out of the miners' heads, the news of Radetsky's death, when announced, seemed to stir the heart of every creature on the goldfield.  He had had a short lucid interval before his last agony, had lamented that he could not have died for Poland, but rejoiced that the blood of the last male of the ancient house of Radetsky had been shed for liberty.  Every male of his line for three generations had perished by sword or bullet in the field in freedom's cause; and though he would leave his bones in this far land, the celestial spirit of freedom would hallow his grave.  He thanked his comrades of every nation for their sympathy and noble kindness, and then died calmly and contentedly, believing that when the miners were again aroused to strike for liberty the occasion would always revive the name of Stanislas Radetsky.

That night it was announced in every form of public proclamation that all the honours of a military funeral had been decreed by the Executive of the United Miners to their leader and true comrade deceased, and that every miner was expected to attend ; that the pall-bearers would leave the chapel at noon precisely,

and that the procession would attend the corpse
to the cemetery at Green Point Hill.

Never was such melancholy invitation more
universally acceded to. It is a matter of fact
and history that hardly a creature able to perform or provide locomotion, above the age of
infancy, was absent from the gathering to do
honour to the dead. Every shred and fragment
of black cloth, crape, lace, or calico on the field
was put into requisition that day. From early
morning till mid-day the roads leading into the
township were thronged with crowds so mixed
and various that one would have fancied that
an exodus was about to take place under pressure of national defeat or impending calamity.
Men, women, and children, even to the toddling
bairn and the babe that could not be left at
home, were all there, all with one accord eager
to pay the last poor tribute of respect to the
gallant exile who had lived in peace and good-
will for long years unpretendingly and honourably with his humble comrades, and had now
sealed with his blood his devotion to freedom
and justice.

For long hours crowds pressed round his
humble abode where this last descendant of the

proud house of Radetsky had passed away, gazing with strong feeling and even with tears upon the calm face of the dead. The haughty regular features were still. There was a frown upon the tameless brow; they could hardly believe that the bright eagle eye had ceased to flash beneath the heavy lids which had been lovingly closed. It seemed hard to think that a form so highly vitalised, so infused through every nerve with eager force and restless energy, *could die*—could lie cold, motionless, unheeding of the hum and stir and beating hearts of the multitude around, whose pulses he knew so well how to stir with his wild, earnest, defiant words.

It was even so. The delicately moulded but sinewy hand was nerveless now, the hot pulse stilled, the tender, fearless heart cold in death. The tongue that could denounce or defy, persuade or command, was silent for evermore. The brave ally of the weak and the oppressed, the friend of the needy, the brother of the forlorn and deserted, had passed away to the land where truth is crowned and justice reigns eternal.

There was nothing left but to turn away and

weep, and to tread with slow sad steps the familiar track to the grassy pine-shaded cemetery on the rocky hill. The dead man was carried to the chapel in his coffin by four compatriots—for the sons of betrayed Poland were numerous among the cosmopolitan roving gold-seekers, that great wave of humanity which first rolled from western and southern Europe to America in the days of the Californian wonder-treasures, thence to the half-fabulous land of the Antipodes.

There Father O'Rourke, an unobtrusively pious priest, who had never ceased to warn his flock against their illegal action and rash deeds, but had not quitted his post, read the prayers appointed over him. Again the coffin was raised on the shoulders of the pall-bearers, and slowly and mournfully the whole vast procession took their way to the pine-crested hill, where the Commissioner's fancy had decreed that the dead should lie. Behind the pall-bearers came a long array of vehicles—buggies, phaetons, dog-carts, express-waggons, every conceivable kind of carriage in use in the neighbourhood. Then, two and two, a thousand horsemen, winding in an immensely long undulating line.

The guilds and brotherhoods and societies walked in array, all carrying the regalia of their orders, and rich with banners and plumes. Then an army of dark-clothed miners, followed by a confused multitude—men, women, and children.

Had any one visited the Oxley township that day, it must have looked like a fabled city of the dead, so thoroughly deserted was it. The day was cloudless and bright. The faint breeze caused the forest trees to quiver and rustle, the river murmured and rippled all un-heeding. How strange a contrast with the day's bright tints, the sombre dark-hued crowd with their dread burden in the fore-front, and the 'Dead March' in *Saul* pealing and rever-berating through the hushed silence of the forest.

But a few weeks since, and he whom they mourned had been strong, eager, tameless by toil or ease, hunger or thirst, fear or favour. Temperate always, yet patient at his rude labour, there yet always seemed within the man a smouldering fire of hatred of injustice, of resistance to tyranny, of sympathy for the weak, defiance for the strong oppressor, which needed but a breath of sympathy or antagonism to fan into the red glowing blaze of revolt and resistance. His lot was latterly cast amid untoward surroundings, but of such material have the world's unforgotten brave, her patriots, heroes, and martyrs, been ever constructed.

Hours passed of the clear, bright winter day, and still the procession seemed winding along the road to the cemetery. When, however, the corpse with its attendant mourners, with the priest, and the leaders of the procession, were seen to enter the cemetery, the line of march was broken up, and in open order those who were mounted rode at speed for the gates, while those on foot strove by short cuts and quickened pace to make up for other deficiencies.

When the grave was opened and the coffin lowered, the priest raised his voice and commenced the service for the dead. Every knee was bent, every voice was hushed, and the great crowd inside the enclosure and as far as the eye could reach knelt as one man, honouring in that hour him who, in their estimation, had fallen for the sacred cause of liberty and for his fellow-men.

More than half of those who thus bent the knee did not belong to the Romish faith. But this was an occasion when all men are equal in the sight of God, the Supreme Ruler of the Universe, before whom the wise and the unlearned are alike helpless, alike dumb. May none ever do anything more unbecoming to their own faith than to act as we did that day —falling on our knees by the grave of the man all had loved, and praying to God for his soul's rest.

In a few moments more the solemn and touching service was ended. The cemetery was speedily emptied, the crowd broke up, and each section of the assembly sought its home, those who were mounted returning at a pace very different from that of the morning.

# CHAPTER XXIII

OF course the Government of the colony of New South Wales was not inclined to rest peaceably while its laws were being broken, its officers withstood, and inoffensive foreigners violently treated and driven out by force of arms. No one expected that for one moment. The British ensign, since it first floated to the breeze above the scarped sandstone natural fortresses of Sydney, has ever truly symbolised the good faith and firm rule of the parent land. The will of the people has never been pandered to by the Ministries of the day, ever justly dreading that weakness of the Executive which has been the curse of all lands where its evil growth has been fostered.

No sooner had the official despatches reached Sydney than efforts were promptly made to march to the scene of revolt every available soldier, sailor, marine, and volunteer that could be impressed for the expedition.

By good luck, as some persons thought, a man-of-war was reposing peacefully in the harbour, and within twenty-four hours her gallant captain, his force of marines and blue-jackets, with a couple of guns for siege purposes if necessary, had started with the regiment then in barracks and a strong body of volunteers, for a three-hundred-mile march across the Blue Mountains to the head-waters of the Oxley.

It was a toilsome and not over-pleasant journey. There were no transmontane railways in those days, and many obstacles had to be encountered. The weather was cold, even frosty, as one of the sailors of the *Collingwood* discovered when, having committed an act of pillage, he was promptly court-martialled, tied up to a gun, and received three dozen at 6.30 A.M., to the surprise and consternation of the provincials.

However, though ranking beneath Sir Charles Napier's march through Scinde and other feats of endurance, the difficulties of the march were gallantly met and at length sur-mounted. The army, with guns in position, colours flying, and all the pomp and circumstance of glorious war, marched into the Oxley, and took up a position in the rear of the camp, which had been promptly vacated at the rumour of their approach. With them also returned the whole available police force of the district, accompanied, of course, by Mr. Merlin, Mr. Bagstock, and the sergeant. Captain Blake, who was an old friend of the colonel of the 70th, accompanied that regiment, and rejoiced in renewing his mess recollections and the routine of military life.

As for our rebels, they were much disorganised, and as usual intestine feuds had weakened their organisation. Now that the Chinese had been driven forth and the coveted shallow ground placed in the possession of the legitimate miner, the revolutionary business became distinctly a bore. Much time was wasted by the committee elected to administer justice in the matter of mining disputes. It was wearisome enough to listen to the interminable technical details which are indispensable in mining evidence, and apparently not more satisfaction was produced than of old. The suitors quarrelled and wrangled and accused

the mining assessors of being partial, pre-
judiced, or indeed interested — charges which
no one ever thought of bringing against the
Commissioner or the magistrates.

Their total freedom from aristocratic and
official guidance was not such a grand thing
after all.    It was a white elephant, costly,
troublesome, and increasingly difficult to support.

The great body of the mining population
was too intelligent, well - intentioned, and respectable to succeed brilliantly in revolt.   They
had no special aims of their own to serve, no
restless ambitions, no covetousness of wealth
or power for their own sakes.   All that they
wished was that they might be permitted to
enjoy their fascinating occupation in peace, and
that no hated aliens of inferior races should be
suffered to swarm among their camps, and
spread themselves locust - fashion over their
beloved shallow ground — the prize and blue
riband, as it were, of the toilsome mining life.

And now the task was done, they did not
longer care to play out the farce of government
and police administration.   After all it was
better done by people trained to it and paid

for it. All this gratis magisterial work was a nuisance, and dreadfully expensive in time to the few leading miners into whose hands it fell. Such considerations as these were not suffered to sleep for want of iteration and support by the Major and myself, as well as by scores of men of the same calibre and higher logical acumen, of whom the diggings are full.

Fortunately little blood had been spilled. Except Radetsky, no man's life had been sacrificed. The Chinese, no doubt, had been beaten and badly handled. Sonora Joe, and some of his friends who had seen scalps taken, it is feared shore more than closely in severing pigtails. They could bring actions for damages.

Now that the soldiers had come, it became necessary either to resolve to stand committed to an obstinate and bloody contest, sure to be a losing one in the end, or to lay down their arms.

For many reasons it was thought advisable to consider seriously of the latter course.

With the military and naval forces now near at hand, it was reported that the colonial secretary, Sir Charles Camden, a veteran politician,

a native-born Australian, and a most able
diplomatist, had accompanied them.   This was
considered by the moderate party to be a
felicitous circumstance.   Sir Charles was a
man whom his enemies called the High Priest
of the Expedient, and his friends knew to be
uniformly successful when a dangerous difficulty needed the solvents of tact and timely
concession.   It is just possible to fancy that
his occasional lack of uncompromising firmness
led to political catastrophes.   But once let
the imbroglio be fairly developed and disaster
imminent, there did not live in the southern
hemisphere a man so effective in unravelling
the tangled skein and reducing the chaotic
elements to order and safety.

On a certain Monday morning, therefore,
the advanced guard of the force, consisting
of six companies of the 70th, marched with
colours flying and bugles blowing into the
camp reserve.   Here they were presently
joined by the volunteers, finally by the sailors
and marines, the former dragging with them
their two formidable pieces of ordnance.

To their astonishment they were loudly
cheered on taking up position in front of the

line, as they coolly unlimbered and got their
artillery ready for action.

Before all this took place, however, Sir
Charles had driven quietly into town in a
dog-cart, with his servant behind him, while
the plain, middle-sized, quietly-dressed man
who sat behind, and who slipped down and
mingled easily with the crowd, was a distinguished colonel of engineers, then in Sydney
on leave, who had joined the expedition as a
matter of interesting inquiry and novel experience.

When it was found that there was no
disposition on the part of the miners to con-
tinue their independent government, but that
the camp and other Imperial strongholds were
delivered up in good order and condition, even
with the addition of a couple of prisoners in
one of the cells awaiting trial for petty larceny,
negotiations were established between Sir
Charles Camden and the leading representative miners. The upshot of this was that
the Government revised the Goldfields Regulations, making, among other changes and
alterations, by the Commissioner's advice, one
which rendered illegal any occupation by

Chinese for the purpose of gold mining upon
auriferous ground which had not been worked
and abandoned by Europeans for the full term
of three years.

This satisfied the mining community, and
healed the rankling sore which threatened such
dangerous if not fatal results to the body
politic.    Shallow ground and new ground
would henceforth be hermetically sealed to
the Mongolian.   The virtuous Caucasian pro-
prietor and his followers of the true faith
would be henceforth enabled to possess their
souls in peace.   I am not quite sure whether
our ally, the Emperor of China, upon whom
we forced our enterprising opium-traders in
and around certain jealously closed ports,
would have considered it strictly in accordance
with international justice.   But it was a measure
highly expedient, if not vitally necessary.   For
that reason, or because it was 'a far cry to
Lochow,' or, in other words, a long way from
the Oxley to Pekin, no protest on the part of
his Celestial Highness reached us.

Sergeant M'Mahon made a few arrests,
including some of the leading rioters, against
whom evidence of violence or special ill-

treatment of Chinese was forthcoming, and
they were duly committed for trial at the next
ensuing Quarter-Sessions. They were held
to bail, and duly tried. But the juries refused
to bring them in guilty, and with their discharge ended peacefully the great Oxley
Flat *émeute*, now only of fading historical
interest.

We, individually, were unaffectedly sorry
when the troops left. There was an old comrade or two of the Major's among the officers,
and though they chaffed him as having been
found in arms against the Sovereign, and so
on, we held high revelry, and had many
pleasant excursions and rambles while the
sailors and soldiers remained. Mr. Bright was
also a favoured guest, and his warlike re-
miniscences gave the allied warriors much
material for surprise and thought. He always
averred that his counsels and influence with
Sir Charles, to whom he was intimately known,
contributed materially to the final and effective
settlement of the question at issue. With the
departing troops a gold escort service was improvised, which carried down all the gold
which had accumulated, to the joint relief of

bankers and depositors, among which last we
were numbered.

The time had passed so quickly during all
these abnormal and exciting proceedings, that
we were quite surprised to find that our appeal
case was on in the Supreme Court of New
South Wales, held in Sydney.

Dr. Bellair went down in person to represent
his friends and clients.   But all his eloquence
and fiery declamation availed him nothing with
the modern Rhadamanthus and his periwigged
compeers.   The appeal was dismissed, with so
swingeing an amount of costs as against the
appellants that all thought of testing the merits
of the case further was peremptorily abandoned.
No higher court of judicature remained, except
the Imperial Privy Council, with which ultimate
legal resort, or indeed with the fraternity generally, the principal backers (on the Doctor's
having tentatively defined its functions) refused, 'in Anglo-Saxon of the strongest kind
that's made,' to have further truck or trouble.

Thus at length we found ourselves, after all
our delays and anxieties, in indisputable possession of the celebrated and coveted No. 4.
Our Oxley claim was doing so well that we

felt a slight *embarras des richesses*, but after a
solemn council we decided to send Cyrus and
Joe back, with authority to put on men and
place the claim once more in full working order.
Mrs. Yorke at once commenced to pack up her
effects ; stating at the same time that she was
'full up of the Oxley, which was a rowdy, dis-
agreeable goldfield as ever she was on, not a
patch on old Yatala for comfort, which she had
two minds never to have come away from, only
Cyrus was a man that always wanted looking
after, being that soft and good-natured as anybody might get round him, and run him to
spend money on all sorts of foolishness, as well
as taking shares in every duffer-lead on the
field, as even his own children picked up from
the shepherds was no good.'

While this full explanation of the defects
of his character was proceeding, much to our
amusement, though from our intimate knowledge of our mate's ways we had little to learn,
Mrs. Yorke was working away most energetic-
ally and effectively, while Cyrus smoked his
pipe with an air of philosophical calmness, as
if his wife was opening up a subject of entirely
new points of interest and abstract bearing.

As soon as we had finished the next wash-up I was to go back to Yatala to supervise the management, audit the accounts, and so on, finally arranging for the carrying on of the two branches of our mining partnership, either of itself immensely lucrative, but none the less needing both energy and careful guidance to result in the splendid financial success we now so plainly saw before us.

.          .          .          .          .          .

In a couple of weeks, having had the satisfaction of seeing a goodly store of the unmistakable metal lying on the rude wooden receptacle of the machine, after all the clay and water-worn pebbles and extremely yellow water had been finally run off, thence transferred to a camp kettle and carefully banked, I returned to Yatala to look up Cyrus and No. 4.

The old town, though kept on its legs principally by the frontage claims of which ours was a sample, was comparatively deserted. Whole streets and suburbs appeared to have vanished, and the grass was growing on many a floor where we had been on good terms with the occupants, and occasionally spent festive hours.

Some of the old identities still survived, and among them were Mrs. Mangrove and old John, who had so loyally backed us in our days of adversity.   That speculative but forecasting matron was overjoyed at our return.

'I always stuck to it, Harry and his crowd would come out all straight some day,' she said exultingly ; 'didn't I, John, old man ?   I always said the Major would drop in lucky, for all those yaller books of his.   Nothing like taking it cool and not breaking out in the drink line when the party was down in the mouth for a spell, as one might say.   Some men would have been on their backs for a week at a stretch with the hard times you've gone through.   But I always did like a party with a smart clever woman like that little Mrs. Yorke of yours among 'em to do for 'em and keep 'em straight. And your sweetheart at home, Harry, she brought you luck, you may swear.   I suppose you'll go back and marry her when the claim's worked out and the Oxley regular done up, and forget all of us roughs here.'

'I shall never forget you, old woman,' I said, 'you may depend your life on that, nor John either ; so make your mind easy.   See

what a present I'll send you out from the old
country.'

'I think John and me had better go home
too,' said Mrs. Mangrove. 'You might get
another rough turn, and want somebody as
knew you to be your backer again, Harry, my
boy.'

'No, no! none of that,' quoth John, laying
his pipe provisionally on his knee, a habit of
his on the rare occasions when he thought fit
to confirm or contravene the course of the executive department. 'England's too far off to
follow a rush, and too dashed cold into the
bargain. I couldn't stand it now.'

'What! worse than Hokitiki or Kiandra?'
said his experienced helpmate. 'Don't you
remember our getting snowed up on the Long
Plain, and having to feed the horses on the flour
they was a-packin'?'

'Yes, that was rather a close thing,' assented
John. 'We was pretty near used up when
they found us. I should ha' been dead only
for that spare flannel petticoat of yours; but
there's no get away in the old country, that's
what I look at, and no gold neither, except what
you brings in your breeches pocket. I reckon

we'll stick to old New South Wales, for as bad
as it is, while our time lasts.'

'I reckon we may as well,' said his superior
officer, 'unless anything happen to you, and
then up stick and clear out, John. I never
could fancy being shovelled in here; that
graveyard always puts me in mind of a
shallow rush on purchased land, where they
make you fill in all the duffer shafts. We
never did no good on purchased land, did we,
John?'

'Well, if that's all as troubles ye, old woman,
you'd better get the Commissioner to register
you a fancy business allotment there and you
can make the improvements all ready for the
last decision, fancy marble crib, headstone and
all complete. Only some o' those fossickers
would come rooting round with a dish after
shower, prospecting, like, for any specimens ye
might have taken with ye.'

'Don't talk of such dreadful things,' said
our usually unprejudiced *marchande*, shuddering superstitiously. 'As sure as your name's
John Mangrove, some one will lose the number of their mess before the week's out. I've
known it happen a score of times before now.

You'd better be off to your bed afore you make any more pleasant remarks.'

This broke up the sitting, and we all departed; but strange and grotesque as were the ideas suggested, none of us treated the presentiment with such indifference as to jest upon it. Unlikely as were all the circumstances, and superior as was our position to what it had been of late years, I could not help confessing to an involuntary feeling of gloom and boding fear which I tried in vain to shake off.

On the morning after the conversation recorded we were hard at work arranging for future business. The claim was too good to be left alone for more than a day or two at a time, and the wages-men, like all other day labourers, were none the worse for personal supervision. Cyrus Yorke and three miners were detailed for the day-shift, and went on accordingly after breakfast, the others, with Joe Bulder, having their allotment of labour during the hours of darkness.

On our way to the claim our large friend was in unusual spirits. He had made a match with his horse for the following Saturday afternoon holiday, and flattered himself that his

antagonist had underrated the pace and breeding of his nag.   Like most Australians, and
one Blount in the service of the late lamented
Lord Marmion, Cyrus was a 'sworn horse-
courser.'   He was, indeed, a thoroughly good
judge, and, heavy as he was, a first-class rider
and whip.   He had picked up a thorough-bred
horse, which had found his way, more or less
feloniously and unlawfully, into the Yatala
pound, and had been sold out, poor, ragged,
and studiously disfigured, for considerably
under his value.   By New South Wales law,
and indeed by that of nearly all the other
colonies, a pound sale gives a perfect and
indefeasible title to any animal sold therefrom,
no matter what equilarcenous acts may have
led to his incarceration.

So Saracen, a great upstanding, weight-
carrying bay, 'tower of strength, with a turn of
speed,' a son of the well-known imported English blood sire Saladin, had at second-hand
become his property for the sum of thirty
pounds and a wash-dirt cart.

It was more than whispered that Larry
Lurcher had stolen the animal, then in training,
out of his stables on a great breeding station to

the north, ridden him a hundred miles by day-dawn, and 'worked' him with the aid of, as it turned out, *untrustworthy* confederates into the Yatala pound.   One of these said confederates was to buy him out of the pound and hand him over to 'the first robber' directly afterwards, thus to evade suspicion.

This worthy person *did* buy the horse, but utterly declined to convey him by legal receipt to his fellow-thief.   Larry of course could not explain the transaction sufficiently to regain his property by legal process.   So the unjust one triumphed, and unblushingly resold Saracen (for his name had leaked out) for just double what he had given, and had the wash-dirt cart, with fifteen pounds more to the good—Mr. Merlin notwithstanding.   This official was in possession of the facts of the case—the name of the former owner of the horse, the night upon which he had been stolen, the distance he had been ridden, and lastly the name of the thief. But he had *no evidence* to connect the adroit receiver with the stolen property.   There was not material for 'a case.'   So he had to acquiesce in hard fortune, and to smile upon the felon, mentally reserving him for a day of wrath.

Since Cyrus Yorke had become possessed of
Saracen he had improved immensely, and was
now 'fit to go for a man's life,' as he said.    I
never saw Cyrus in better spirits, though to do
him justice, hard fortune or good, he was
always ready to enjoy himself, holding to such
proverbs as 'Care killed a cat,' ' A short life and
a merry one,' ' It will be all one in a hundred
years,' and other wise saws tending to decry
undue forethought and anxiety for the morrow.

' My word,' he said, just before I put my leg
into the bight of the rope and prepared to
descend the one hundred feet of our shaft,
'we're getting rich now, and no mistake.    I
never expected to see the cash rolling in, hand
over hand, like this here.    I feel as if I'd more
than I know what to do with already.    If it
wasn't for the old woman and the kids I'd cut
it, sell out, and buy a few farms on the Hawkesbury as would keep me the rest of my life.    If
I win this match with Saracen on Saturday, I
don't know as I won't do it now.'

' Don't do anything rash, Cyrus,' I said ;
' better see the claim worked out, and then you
can bank your money and live like a gentleman.'

# CHAPTER XXIV

'THAT's all very well, Cyrus,' I said, after a while, 'but you must either do one thing or another. This racing doesn't go well with digging. You'll have to be brought up before the Commissioner under the "efficient working" clause and fined, or else we'll put a man on and charge you a pound a day. We're all sticking to our fight and you're beginning to jack up.'

'All right, Harry,' he said good-humouredly, 'don't be afraid, old man, I'm good for a year's work yet, anyhow. Wait till I get down directly and I'll show you how a native can handle a pick. That Joe Bulder's a good man, but he can't do the day's work I can turn out, though he is a Britisher. Can he now?'

'He certainly cannot,' I conceded, 'nor any other man in the claim; only you're not quite so regular as he is.'

'You get out of my way, then, old Parson Harry. I'll be down directly after you send the rope up; don't be long. Lower away.'

I slid softly down with my foot in the bight of the rope below the rim of mother-earth, and in the requisite number of seconds was safely on the shaft bottom, from which I retreated into a sideling gallery called 'a drive,' and was about to question a wages-man as to how they were doing when I heard a sudden, rushing, unwonted sound, terminating in a horrible dull thud upon the hard earth at the bottom of the shaft. How my heart sickened! How did my blood run cold as I *knew* it must be a *man*! I rushed to the shaft. Several men from the other interior workings met there. We raised the man, for it was one, and little but the outward presentment of what was once Cyrus Yorke. He was not insensible; better had he been so. His first words were, 'Oh, my God! my back, my back!'

When we raised him his whole frame was nerveless, dreadfully limp, and incapable of being supported in an upright position. Then we found, amid his groans and involuntary cries, that both legs were broken, an arm, with possibly internal injuries superadded.

He was fastened in an impromptu chair and drawn up with the aid of another miner, who went up with him, holding him as tenderly as a brother. It is in the time of real disaster, of mortal hurt, that one sees the true value of the manly heart. Little is said, there are no professions, but the proverbial feminine tenderness is often equalled by that of the chance comrades whose ordinary speech would lead a superficial observer to infer that not one grain of sentiment could abide with the rough exterior and ruder utterances.

Cyrus had full possession of his senses, and in answer to a question as to how he fell, groaned out, ' I forgot the sprag.' In the exuberance of his spirits he had jumped on to the rope and neglected to see that the wooden wedge, which when placed in the iron roller arrests and acts as a brake to the outrunning rope, was in its place. The unchecked rope ran through the roller with tremendous velocity, and poor Cyrus reached the bottom of the shaft almost as rapidly as though he had thrown himself down it.

There was no hope from the first. A messenger was sent to tell his wife that the earth
had fallen in, and that her man was badly hurt.
This is the most common phase of mining
accident ; for this every miner's wife is more or
less prepared. In many instances they do not
terminate fatally. There is generally some
hope ; but poor Mrs. Yorke fortunately dreaded
the worst, and cried out when she saw the little
procession—

'Oh, Cyrus! oh, my man! He'll never get
off his bed. I dreamed of it the other night.
If they've got to carry him, he's a dead man. I
know before they tell me.'

However, she braced herself to the task,
and with dry eyes was soon busied in making
ready for him the bed, which, though in a poor
tent, was neater and more scrupulously tended
than in many a grander abode.

As the four men approached with the bark
stretcher, upon which lay the huge frame of the
magnificent athlete who had gone forth that
morning in all the frolic spirits of youth rejoic-
ing in his strength, there was already a small
crowd collected near the tent door. His wife
came forward, and giving one rapid despairing

glance threw herself upon a low chair and covered her face with her hands. Then she walked forward, and bending down kissed the pale face of the death-stricken miner, already tortured by the spasms of mortal agony.

'Never mind, old woman,' he said, with an effort to make his big voice sound cheery and careless as of old, 'don't take on so. The doctor won't mend me, I'm thinking; but you'll have enough for your share of the claim to keep you and the kids for your lives.'

'Don't talk of the claim. I wish we'd never seen it. Oh, my God! have pity on me! Lay him down gently on the bed, please. Why can't I die too?'

There was no need to ask them to lay their ghastly burden down gently. A dozen willing hands were at once proffered, and as lightly as a babe by its mother was the injured man laid upon the bed he was never to quit alive.

Then almost mutely, but with looks and gestures full of heartfelt commiseration, such as could not have been surpassed in the most polished society of the old world, the crowd reverently and heedfully went on its way and left the mourners to their sorrowful duties.

The nearest doctor was at once sent for. He came with little delay ; but beyond swathing up the wounded man, so that present pain was minimised, nothing could be done.

The wife looked long and searchingly at his impassive countenance, but found there no hope, alas !

'How long shall I have my senses, doctor ?' said poor Cyrus.

'Forty-eight hours, perhaps,' said the man of sickness, wounds, and death. How many death-beds had he seen ! 'You had better make any arrangements to-morrow, in case of accident. If you feel the pains coming on badly, take some of the draught I leave you, but not unless you can't do without it. Good-day !'

I walked out to the road with the doctor, and as far as the nearest hotel, no great distance.

'No chance of recovery, I suppose, doctor ?' I said tentatively.

'My dear fellow, he has hurts enough to kill all four of you—severe internal injuries, fractured spine, broken thighs, arm, bah ! he's a dead man now. Sensible woman, his wife—pity.'

'Poor Cyrus, it's a frightfully sudden end. What will you take, doctor?'

'Brandy, I think—three star.'

All the next day we watched over our poor comrade. Though the pain which he suffered was at times agonising to the limit of human endurance, he was perfectly conscious, and in full possession of his senses.

'That's what makes it so hard to bear,' he said, in one of the intervals when he lay calmed by the powerful narcotic draught, after a paroxysm of unusual fierceness. 'Here am I took, accidental like, all through a minute's cursed carelessness, and me as never had a day's illness, or knowed what it was to be sick or sorry, not once in my life afore. And just as I had my pile pretty well made, so as we'd no call to be grizzlin' and bustin' ourselves for money as long as we lived. Well,' he said reflectively, after a pause, ' I haven't been what folks call a religious cove, but I never wished anybody any harm, and I never done a mean act in my life. And I *do* feel it hard—precious hard—to be rubbed out like this, after followin' the diggings so long, just as I've made the first rise.

Towards nightfall he felt easier, and as he lay with his wife's hand in his, one might have hoped, but for the cruel irreparable shattering of his whole frame, that a favourable change was at hand.    He, however, mistrusted it himself.

'You've been a good wife to me, little woman,' he said to his wife, who now sat looking at him with a fixed gaze of grief, as if the fount of tears was dry, 'and I've not behaved bad to you, that is, as far as I knowed how. When I'm gone, you stick to your shares in the claims till they're clean worked out, and then you go and settle down on the Hawkesbury, where we both was reared, and buy a good farm, and eddicate the poor kids well.    And if you marry again, as women mostly does, and I don't see why you shouldn't, you pick a sensible, steady chap, as'll take care of you and them.    I sha'n't have nothin' to say agin it.    And now, kiss me, old woman, and bring in the poor young uns and the babby, bless his little round mug, for them pains is a-comin' on agin, and they won't have their father much longer, I'm afeared.'

It was even so. An hour later a merciful delirium set in, and during the long night through Cyrus never recovered consciousness —talking mostly of his early days, among the maize fields of the old river, where so many of the early colonists were reared.

At dawn he passed away; and when the miners went forth to their daily work that morning, the giant frame of him whom all had known in robust health and spirits but two short days before, lay cold and stiff for evermore.

We buried him near Radetsky, whom he had followed to the grave, little deeming that he himself was so soon to be laid beside him, and a crowd of mourners only inferior in number to those who formed the death march in honour of the patriot exile paid the last tribute of respect to the big, jolly, generous comrade whom they all knew so well.

As for Mrs. Yorke, she refused all comfort for a while, attending to her household tasks mechanically, but seeming as one whose mental faculties had received a numbing blow. By degrees, however, she rallied, and so far resumed her former nature as to resent a proposal made to her to go 'down the country,' as she

expressed it, and settle in a quiet country town
with her children.

' Poor Cyrus said I was to stop and see how
the claims washed up till the very end,' she said,
'and so I shall as long as they're worth sticking
to. I've followed the diggings so long, as I
should be lost at any other life ; so I'll stop on
and do for you boys, just as I've always done,
till the party's broke up. There's plenty of
good hard work, and that'll keep me from
thinkin' too much and maybe losin' the little
wits I have.'

So Mrs. Yorke abode with the party, knowing that she was among friends and brothers,
and that her children were under the protection
of the whole goldfield, every man in which
would have gone far to aid them in any way.
She gradually became her old, cheery, sharp-
spoken, energetic self again, and matters went
on, as is the world's wont, with a gradually
decreasing memory of the big, easy, good-
humoured husband and father whom she used
to order about with almost as little ceremony as
the children.

As soon as I had reason to believe that No.
4 could be trusted to manage itself without my

supervision, I placed Joe Bulder in charge and returned to the Oxley. There was no very great difficulty in arranging poor Cyrus Yorke's affairs. He had, luckily for himself, taken a fancy to have his will made a couple of years before, being so much taken with the celerity with which Mr. Markham drew up that important document for a fellow-miner *in extremis*, that he got that energetic gentleman to write out one exactly like it for him, leaving everything to his wife, as had his old friend, and actually signed it.

This was most fortunate, and saved all bother with the Curator of Intestate Estates and the necessity of commission to Mr. Bagstock—a result which that gentleman feelingly deplored. We had then only to place Mrs. Yorke's share of the dividends in the bank to her credit after each washing-up, and the poor thing knew to a fraction how much was added to her previous very respectable capital.

After I had returned to the Oxley, and these affairs, revolutionary and otherwise, were done and over, and we had time to think over matters in a calm and unexcited way, it occurred to the Major and myself one night as very strange that Jack Bulder should have taken such very particular care to keep himself out of the whole imbroglio.

'The very thing I should have expected him to have gone in tooth and nail for,' said the Major. 'He has often inveighed against the tyranny and harshness of the officials in the early days of mining, more particularly in Victoria, and occasionally shown an amount of ferocity that surprised me. Now, all through this row he has kept steadily to his work, avoided all meetings, almost ran the risk of being considered a traitor to the cause by some of the hot-headed rioters. Depend upon it, he has a good reason for keeping so quiet.'

'He has shown his sense,' I said. 'There were many good reasons for keeping out of all this unfortunate affair. I wish others had thought the same.'

'Yes, but what I mean is, that he had some feeling beyond that of common prudence which would not have swayed such a savage beggar as he is when his blood is up. There is some mystery, I'll swear.'

'There is some mystery about every digger,' I replied. 'There is nothing wonderful about

that.    If one could only know the real history
of nine-tenths of the people that we pass in the
street or work alongside of for years, there
would   be   the   material   for   more   startling
romances than all the fiction-weavers in Europe
could manufacture in a decade.'

'When one comes to think of it, perhaps if
the Oxley Hotel bars were turned into a veri-
table Palace of Truth instead of one occasionally
witnessing the unveiling of a fragment of the
statue, some novel effects and strong situations
would result.   But none the less do I firmly
believe that our trusty acquaintance and mate
carries about with him a secret as much more
weighty   and   dangerous   than   the   ordinary
miner's possessions as a square foot of nitro-
glycerine is to a canister of powder.'

'If your theory is right about his having a
craving for drink, it will all come out the first
time he has a "burst."   I have noticed his being
restless and excited lately.   It may be that the
enemy is crawling closer to him.'

'Poor devil!   Perhaps it is so.   I must say
I pity those alcoholisers.   It is so hopeless a
case with them.   And they are often such
Bayards in their sane periods.'

'Poor human nature again!' said I; 'but isn't it bed-time?'

More important matters than John Bulder's strange mood had been passed over during the revolutionary and funereal period. So little had I dreamed of aught but war rumours and tragedies of late, that the absence of my accustomed letter from my darling Ruth did not unsettle and ·alarm me, as such an omission usually did.

When I began to reason on the subject I told myself that there was no fixed period for the sending of these priceless missives, and that they were occasionally delayed until the time of my eager expectation had passed.

I had certainly written very fully of late, and had dwelt with more than my usual guarded prudence upon the recent successes and wonderful expectations which had now fallen to our lot.

I had told of my wound, of the robbery of the escort, and of my slow and tedious recovery —all of which facts had elicited the most tender sympathy, the most fervent condolence. I had mentioned, perhaps in somewhat slight and formal manner, the good nursing I had received

from Mrs. Morsley, which had so much tended
to my recovery.   But I had forborne to state
that she was identical with the Jane Mangold
whom Ruth so well recollected at Dibblestowe
Leys.

My reason for this was merely an instinctive
feeling that it was better not to go into the
whole question of poor Jane's Australian career,
and a doubt whether any one in England could
completely understand and accurately gauge
the nature of a goldfield's friendship, all innocent of wrong-doing as such friendships generally are.

Better for all and safer would it have
been had I told the whole unvarnished truth,
and trusted to Ruth's delicate sympathy and
womanly sense of purity to have instinctively
divined the real state of the case.   As it was,
my reticence gave point to the well-nigh fatal
stab to my reputation, aided the death-blow to
my happiness, which my mortal enemy had
known so well how to deal.

I had tortured myself with the sickening
foreboding of evil that sensitive spirits know so
well for some weeks, when a letter came with
the well-known beyond-sea postmark.

To my deep surprise it was in the squire's handwriting.

With mingled feelings I tore it open and read, with confused brain and mist-dimmed eyes, as follows—

# CHAPTER XXV

'ALLERTON COURT.

'SIR—Circumstances have recently been brought to my knowledge connected with your present mode of life in Australia which have entirely changed my opinion of your character.

'Without further alluding to facts, with which I have been made acquainted through the correspondence of a resident at the Oxley diggings and former acquaintance (I enclose the communication), I may state here that I feel myself precluded from all future friendship or association with you.

'Deeply painful as it has been to me and others to decide thus irrevocably, you must be aware that your conduct leaves me no alternative as a father, as a gentleman. May God forgive you. I should be false to my heart's truest feelings if I could add that I did.—Yours obediently, GEOFFRY ALLERTON.

'Hereward Pole, Esq.,
'The Oxley, N. S. Wales, Australia.'

More than once had I turned and returned this fatal scroll, like one who doubts and fears of doom irrevocable, spirit-crushing, eternal.

What foulest slander, what devilish falsehood could have led to this astounding change in the warm-hearted old squire? And if he and his trusting charitable wife believed—as they must have done—the hateful lying slander, what would be the feelings of my pure, gentle, true-hearted Ruth?

And could she desert me at the first whisper of the breath of calumny, she whom I had known to be not less gentle than steadfast? Did I not remember with the vividness of yesterday our walk near the upland terrace along the beech avenue, our youthful sympathy with the Master of Ravenswood, and her scorn of the too easily swayed Lucy Ashton?

As I sat staring at vacancy, rigid with despair and hate of my enemy—for who but Algernon Malgrade had, through some emissary near his old abode, worked all this misery and ruin—I could yet see Ruth's calm eye and severe features as she expressed her belief in the fond faith and clinging adherence to an absent lover, noblest, most exalted attributes of womanhood. Covering my face in an agony too deep for words, well-nigh too great for human endurance, I took comfort from the recollection.

Again and again I re-read the serpent-like scroll which had been cast into my Eden of love and faith, whence I was now, it would appear, for ever cast forth. It was addressed to an erstwhile companion and fellow-reprobate, sharer in Malgrade's darkest iniquities, but who, more astute or more fortunate than he, had never been actually convicted of dishonourable conduct, and was therefore still in the enjoyment of his social position. The poisonous extract ran thus—

'I daresay you remember something about that fellow Pole, who migrated to this strange quarter of the globe just before I did. I never liked the confounded prig, but did him the justice to think that he was hard-working and what the world calls respectable. Still I think poor old Allerton, who was ass enough to allow that nice daughter of his to become engaged to him, ought to know that he has been living in the most open manner with a woman named Morsley, who left her husband to nurse him when he received a wound in the escort robbery, and has remained with him ever since. She was said to have been a *tendresse* of his when he was playing at farming with her father, old Mangold, in Kent. People don't mind that sort of thing here, and *I* am not straitlaced, as you know, but I never was a sanctimonious hypocrite, and I can't stand fellows who sail under false colours.'

This artfully concocted missile had not failed of its effect. Like the frail dart, the keen point of which has been steeped in the festering relics of the charnel-house, the merest scratch was sufficient to rankle and inflame into a mortal wound. 'The death of hope, love, friendship, all that is, except mere breath,' had followed. Should I ever be able to refute the calumny? Should I ever be afforded an opportunity to clear myself of this subtle, deadliest accusation? For the arch-assassin and conspirator in the matter was difficult to reach. We were already known to be sworn enemies. To charge him with the villainy, to assail him with reproaches, would serve no good end. He would probably reply with his polished, imperturbable sneer, well gratified to find that the barbed arrow had gone home. For an actual hand-to-hand conflict the time and place were not fitting. Men did not carry arms at our diggings, and though I felt as if I could have crushed every bone in his body, yet I knew that he was an adept at every kind of athletic exercise, and that an attack by me could only end in an unseemly scuffle and a separation by the adjoining bystanders, with an ultimate appeal to the police-office. Satisfaction was not to be obtained in that way. I must bide my time. He might yet be incriminated in the escort robbery. Merlin was following up the trail like a sleuth-hound. I should yet see him in the dock, thence to receive the full measure of his deserts.

A month passed. How I bore up under my burden I cannot tell. None can ever know. I was fortunate in having the inestimable distraction of full and exhausting bodily toil, which to the strong man, whose muscular power will bear the strain, supplies an anodyne to which none other is comparable. To the Major, who shared all my secrets, though I had not been put into full possession of his, I confided my griefs. He was less sardonic than I had ever known him.

'If I were weak enough to make an exception in favour of any daughter of Eve, which I don't say I do,' he answered musingly, 'I should do so in the case of Miss Allerton. She is, perhaps, one of the rare feminine flowerets which a certain consensus of persons of experience have decided to bloom once in a century. Were I in love, like you, which God forbid, I should hope against hope.'

Did the Major sigh? I could not tell. It would be too wonderful were it so. But after delivering himself of this most unusual sentiment, he departed abruptly.

I was approaching a phase of stony despair, which, apparently, no outward occurrences had power to change, when a letter was brought to me on which I instantly descried the long-loved, long-lamented characters of my love.

Had I been sick and like to die? Even in this hour of sanity and security, I fully believe so. That dull, darksome despair of life, the denial of all worth and value in existence, had set in, which kills in some races even as surely as the sword, though silently as the fatal cup. The Lascar casts himself down, saying I shall die, and by the simple exercise of will—hereditarily so directed—even thus *does* die. Why not the hopeless lover?

Never before had I opened one of her dear letters without being pervaded by a feeling of joy and serenity, which seemed as with some supernal influence to dispel the mists of doubt and danger by which my life was environed. Fearing, as I had good reason now to do, lest the *Argosy*, with all my freight of happiness, had hopelessly foundered, I yet had an instinctive reminiscent sensation of the well-remembered gracious influence. Nor was it illusory. Opening the letter with the obstinately-resolved feeling of one who knows that his charter of life or death, the release or the death warrant, lies between those delicate sheets, I read no farther than 'My darling Hereward,' when I threw myself on my knees and kissed the letter again and again in an agony of love and gratitude, as though it bore the pardon of a soul ransomed from the Inferno.

When my throbbing heart and whirling brain would permit me, I addressed myself more collectedly to the closely-written pages, which ran thus—

'I could not send you this before, though I grieved. They tell me all through the delirium of my illness that you would be left in doubt of your own Ruth, and of her love towards you, even after the wicked slander which has so injured you in papa's estimation. For I have been ill, very ill, my darling, and my poor brain is still weak and troubled with the dreadful imaginings which passed through it during the fever.

'But they tell me I am recovering now, and after the change of air which my dearest mother and I are about to take, I feel that I shall be quite well again and able to act with firmness. How much strength of purpose shall I need to cling to my love through good and evil report.

'Oh, what a dreadful thing it is that wicked people should be permitted to work such woe to those who have never injured them.   I have barely heard of this Algernon Malgrade, whose fiendish letter has done all this evil to us. I was merely told that he was a man whom his friends had long cast off, and whose name was infamous in his own neighbourhood.   That he could never have been a friend of yours, and is now a deadly enemy, I can well understand.   And the deadliest foe he has proved himself to be.

'Before I go further I MUST tell you that though I never believed the wicked invention, yet papa's anger, dear mother's sorrow, and my own vexation that any act of yours should have been capable of such a construction, combined to harass me with doubts and to produce the illness from which I have just arisen.   It was also most unfortunate that you did not tell me in your letters after you were wounded that the nurse, to whom I felt so grateful, was Jane Mangold.   Every one knew her here as a handsome flighty girl before she left England, and all were ready to believe the worst of her after the circumstantial falsehood which Mr. Malgrade's friend, whom I shall always consider as bad as himself, circulated.

'But oh, my own Hereward—long loved, only loved that you are, as from the first—I believed in your truth with all my heart and soul; so I do now.   My father's bitter anger and disappointment at what he terms your ingratitude must yield to time and proof of your innocence. Dear mother is again on my side, and thinks he was over-hasty in condemning you unheard.   As for me, I am yours, in love and faith, as long as life lasts; and nothing that I

can imagine would tear you from my heart, though I might
die in the effort to sever myself from you.

'Write at once, calmly and prudently, to dear father
and set yourself right, as you must be able to do, with as
little delay as possible.   When I think that but for this
terrible escort robbery you might even now have been on
your way home, I can hardly bear to think of the wretches
who planned it, and are responsible for all the evils which
have since flowed from the crime.

'Do not lose a moment in calming the fears about
yourself which I constantly entertain, and in proclaiming
your justification before my parents and all the world.   But,
whatever may be their opinion—and I pray that I may not
be deemed wicked for opposing it,—I am and shall be
always, your own                    RUTH ALLERTON.'

I carefully folded up and put away among
my hoarded treasures this the most rare and
precious of them all—the assurance of a
pure and loving woman's devotion.   Encompassed as she was by apparently well-founded
fears and anxieties, by the opposition of her
parents and friends, and the opinion of the
society in which she lived, what courage did
she display !   A difficult measure of antagonism
for one so gentle and tender to withstand.   Yet,
for my sake, she repressed her natural desire to
conform in all respects to the will of those
tender parents with whom her life had been

spent in willing obedience, choosing rather to
trust in the fealty of one who, like me, was
living in a strange land, the sport of wild adventure, of untoward fate, the undefended victim of
calumny.

Whatever love mortal man could give, had
ever given to woman, was her due ; and if ever
man had loved truly and with all the strength
of his being, I, Hereward Pole, was that man.
Why could I not at once take steps and in
person defy my maligners and for ever put to
flight all doubt of my good faith ?    I could
*almost* do it.    If I sold out now and quitted
the goldfields I should leave with a fair fortune,
a respectable competence sufficient to provide
moderately for all my wants in days to come.    But
just now, at the crowning point of fortune, when
*everything*, in a miner's point of view, was in
our favour, it seemed too hard to quit the still
running golden stream and leave to others the
garnering of the wondrous treasures which were
within our grasp.    No ! I had sworn to return
to the land of my forefathers with such a portion
of the golden store of this new world as should
suffice to equip their descendant with something of the old splendour of the ancient house.

I had wrested so much from the dragons which guarded the Hesperides of the south. I would reappear, laden with what would disarm the sneers and purchase for evermore the smiles of the fawning crowd we dignify as society.

Yes! in despite of the weary load of over-worn patience, of the crushing sorrow, never more sharply mordant than now, and the machination of fiends, falsely called men, I would adhere to my first resolution, never departed from, and fight out my life-battle to the close. The stubborn pride which compelled my expatriation forbade a premature return.

Meanwhile all that I could do should be done. I would write both to the Squire and to my own unfaltering high-souled love, placing before them the fullest details, the most minute facts. My exculpation I would leave to a just and merciful God, to my Ruth's tender trust, to her father's honour and plighted word.

And yet, how was I to bear myself towards the ill-fated woman who was so closely, so ominously linked with my fortunes? Was I, with selfish dread of damage, to cast her off at the first storm summons of wave and gathering blast, as seamen, mad with fear or reckless in

despair, cast forth the weaker comrade from an
overladen skiff? Not for even her dear love's
sake, not for the risk of withering up the life
that remained to me, as a flame-scorched scroll,
would I so far dishonour my manhood by the
desertion of a trust.

This late-stricken victim, this forlorn creature,
alone in a world which was thronged with foes
and oppressors, had crept to my feet to die or
to be succoured in sore need in the name of
the old pure friendship of our joyous charmed
youth, and was I to cast her off with calculating
cowardice because her name had been used to
forge a false indictment?

No! by heaven! some men might do this
thing, might hug themselves with the belief that
the seeming cruelty of prudence was but the
duty to themselves and their stainless reputation which all men owe. But might the Lord
do so to me, and more, in the words of the
ancient record of man's earliest tragedies, if I,
Hereward Pole, stooped to so base a shelter
from the storm of calumny which bade fair to
whelm me.

   .    .    .    .    .    .  .

So I betook me to the poor substitute for

the spoken word, which those must ever employ
who look to lighten the wrong which has been
for ages the proverbial doom of the absent.  I
shut myself up, and devoted a long day to the
careful compilation of a record of all that had
occurred between us since I had first seen the
unhappy Jane Mangold in Australia.  I wrote
humbly and patiently to the old Squire, solemnly
pledging my faith as a man and a gentleman,
that no tie existed between us save such as was
almost a necessity of our positions, and which
reflected honour upon our common nature.

I stated finally that she was about to sail for
England shortly, that I had pledged myself to
carry out arrangements to that effect, from
which, of course, he would see that I could not
now draw back, and that as she was returning
to her father's home, he might, if he pleased,
and I earnestly besought him to do so, visit her
at the Leys, and hear from her own mouth the
true facts of the case.  When face to face with
her, I could trust to his clear head and knowledge of the world to unravel any apparent
mystery.

My task over, my despatches sealed and
posted, somewhat of my burning anxiety was

allayed. Some portion of the load was lifted from my soul. I felt nerved to attempt the completion of my errand to this fair land, abstracted as it had been hitherto, as by all the evil genii of an Eastern tale, and yet I had so lately yearned but to cease from penitent, aimless struggling against fate, to sleep the sleep of the tired wayfarer, to lie down and die!

Thus I sought out Jane; told her—for I thought it well to do so—of the coward shaft that had been aimed against two lives. Her old fiery nature blazed fiercely out at Malgrade's treachery.

'Liar and coward that he is!' she cried. 'I could stab him with my own hand. *He* knew it was a lie—none better, but he hates me' (here she blushed painfully) 'not less than he does you. He thought he would ruin us both with the same miserable slander. If I was a man I would tear his false heart out. And yet'—here the whole expression of her face softened and changed—'I only am to blame that my name could ever be used to injure yours, to cause you unhappiness and bring sorrow into your life and of those whom you love. I am indeed a most unhappy creature, born to do evil to my best

friends, to those I love best; and I have at
times a foreboding—oh! so dark and fearful,
when I am long alone—that I shall yet work
misery to you, Hereward Pole—my friend, my
only friend! Why was I born? Why does
God make such women as I have been—oh!
why, why?'

Here her whole frame was shaken by a fit
of passionate weeping, which lasted for some
time before I could interfere to comfort her
and counsel a calm consideration of her future
course. At length she controlled herself by a
painful effort so piteously visible through every
movement of her limbs and features that the
hardest, coldest heart must then have permitted
mercy to temper justice.

Raising her tear‑stained face, and essaying at first vainly to speak, like a child who
attempts to do so after abandonment to passionate grief, she again addressed me—

'I declare, as God hears me, that I would
go away this moment where you would never
hear of me more and no tongue could pierce
this poor bleeding heart afresh, but for one
reason, and one only.'

'Do not do anything so rash or foolish, my

dear Jane. The worst has been said, no further harm can be done—that is one, if a small comfort. I will hasten my trip to Sydney. What I promised you nothing shall induce me to forego. Keep up your spirits, then. A few weeks will see you on your way to Dibblestowe Leys, bless the old place! Once there you can plead my cause, and clear yourself more effectively than all the letters in the world.'

'It is a glimpse of heaven,' she said, 'and do you not think I have been looking forward to it all these weary months as my only reason for living? But for that, as I said, I would start away for Victoria or New Zealand, change my name, and disappear from your life and all that ever heard the name of Jane Mangold. How I wish I had never borne another! But I shall stay, because—because—I am afraid.'

Here so strange and terrible an expression of fear, of mortal fear, passed over her countenance that a half-thought her brain had given way under the strain of her sufferings crossed my mind.

'Jane, Jane,' I said, almost harshly, 'what nonsense is this, what are you afraid of, or of whom?'

'I do not know of whom,' she said in a
strange low voice, with her eyes fixed on
vacancy as one who peers into thick darkness;
'but I have a horrible dread, a kind of waking
dream, of being *murdered*. And oh! how un-
speakably awful, how fearful it must be to be
killed in a second, in some cruel, painful way—
sent to judgment with all one's sins upon one's
head!'

'And who is there to kill you?' I said,
trying but in vain to assume a cheerful tone.
'Of course—well——' here I hesitated; 'but
why talk of impossibilities, these sort of things
are never done?'

'They are done,' she said, still in the same
low, murmuring, unnatural tone. 'Don't you
remember that case of Clara Denver, poor
thing? I saw her laughing carelessly the very
day before. Still I don't think he would do it,
though I used to think so once. Twice I
dreamed of a man in a dark cloak, a sort of
poncho. I could not see his face, but he had
a knife, a horrid knife!' Here she shuddered
and almost gasped for breath. 'I felt its
sharp edge across my throat. Then I
woke, screaming out. Twice I dreamed this.

Do you think dreams are ever sent to warn people?'

'You have been terrifying yourself with fancies and imagining, my poor Jane,' I said, 'until you begin to see visions. Look at the clear sky and the bright sunshine. Where is the need for all this gloom and sadness? You and I are still alive and well in spite of the misery which others have caused us. Let us look facts in the face, do our duty, and trust in God. I must tell Mrs. Yorke to make you walk a little more—you shut yourself up too much.'

'You know I can't go walking about like other people,' she said; 'but you are always good and kind, and I feel better already. I will try and think of nothing—nothing—till you are ready to start for Sydney; and then God may pardon me and give me another chance for happiness in this life. Good-bye!'

She held out her hand instinctively, and then half shyly withdrew it, as if she recognised some additional reason why not even the minor greetings of life should be exchanged between us; then, as I grasped hers, said timidly, 'I suppose we may shake hands, mayn't we?'

I pressed her hand in mute disavowal of the tyranny of the idle or evil-speaking world to bind our every act and speech. As she turned and walked slowly, almost feebly away, I turned away my head, for I could not bear the sight of her altered mien and form, so changed from the bright womanly graces of old days.

It yet wanted some hours of sunset. There was no need for my returning to the claim. I had provided for my share of the work being efficiently performed in my absence. I shrunk from the idea of sitting or lying down aimlessly after the tumult of emotion which I had so recently experienced. I turned my steps towards the forest path which led outwards from the diggings, breasting the slope with rapid stride, and feeling the sunset breeze as it fanned my brow an indescribable relief to a fevered spirit.

I had crossed more than one crest of the slate-strewn ranges, and was threading the close shrubbery of a narrow grassy dell, when I saw the woman whom we knew as Dolores coming along the track. Bareheaded, with rapid pace and eager gesture, she turned at once towards me as her eyes lighted on my approaching figure.

Her head was thrown back ; her black hair, which was loose, fell in great masses down her back.   Her eyes were flashing, and her white even teeth were set closely with a resolved, almost cruel expression.

I thought of passing her without appearing to take notice of her altered mien, but dismissed the idea as I marked her evident distress and agitation.

'Good evening, Mrs. Malgrade,' I said ; 'what's wrong with you ?   Has anything happened ? '

' Happened !' she said, with fierce hate and scorn filling every line of her features, and blazing in her large dark eyes that seemed aglow with unearthly light.   'What should happen to a woman that's bound to Algernon Malgrade but wrong and ill-treatment.   What have you to say of a man that strikes, that beats his wife ?   God help me! I am not THAT, but the miserable woman that bears his name ; and here I swear before God that I will never do so more, or break bread, or live under the same roof with him, if I starve or work my fingers to the bone for it.'

Here the excited woman fell upon her knees

and raised her hands and face to heaven. 'I swear that I, Dolores Lusada, will never more live under the same roof with Algernon Malgrade, or take a morsel of meat or a piece of money from his hand, if I should starve ; and if I do not keep this oath may my brain wither and this hand rot to the shoulder. Look here, Harry,' said she, 'do you see the pretty mark ?' Here I saw that her face was bruised and cut as with a heavy blow. 'And see here ;' she pulled up her sleeve, and on her white round arm was another livid mark that no light stroke ever made. 'And now you despise me. I know you do. Oh, Lord God! that ever I should have come to this !'

Then she threw herself upon the green turf, and covering her face with her hands wept and lamented with so dreadful an agony of tears, as if (in the phrase of childish days) 'her heart would break.'

It was not in my nature to abstain from offering such poor shreds of consolation as I had to bestow to any woman under such stress of circumstances. I certainly distrusted, and in a way disliked, Dolores as much as I could dislike a very beautiful woman, which was not, after all, a very active sentiment.  I was fully aware that she might work me evil, and that to be seen with her would by no means conduce to my social reputation.  For even on goldfields Mrs. Grundy is no obsolete puissance.

I calmed the frantic woman, and partly persuaded her to go to a respectable quiet lodging in Yatala, where she could remain until either she effected a reconciliation with Malgrade, which I knew was highly probable, constituted as women are, or made final arrangements for separation.  Go back at present she would not, nor had I the heart to urge her.

I felt a grim half-bitter smile pass over my features as I said aloud—

'It is Kismet.  Surely I am doomed to be the champion of every distressed dame and damsel on the goldfield.  I am Amadis de Gaul or some other mediæval knight of romance, or perchance Don Quixote himself.  If my heart is reflected in my face, there could scarce be a closer presentment of the knight of the sorrowful countenance.  How the Major will oppress me!'

I had brought matters to this more or less satisfactory stage, and was departing on my own track, leaving her to follow the path to the township, which she knew very well, when a figure crossed the crest of the hill which caused both of us to start instinctively.

It was Algernon Malgrade. I noted the exact moment when he recognised our figures. He checked his pace for an instant, then advanced with a slow indifferent step and studied air of lounging carelessness.

He halted within a yard, and gazed steadfastly in both faces as if to read our very souls. Then he laughed. Devils laugh so. I felt certain of it, though I had, of course, no means of verifying the fact.

# CHAPTER XXVI

' So you didn't drown yourself, *carissima* ? ' he said at length, in his soft vibrating voice, which he could render so melodious at will, ' but have concluded to console yourself and enlist the sympathy of Mr. Hereward Pole. *Je vous en fais mes compliments, monsieur,*' he added, taking off his hat and bowing with an assumption of respectful politeness ; then turning to Dolores, he added, ' I should have thought he had his hands full at present. If madame's temper, not to speak of other attributes, remains unimpaired he will have reason, like me, to bless the hour he first set eyes on you.'

Not prone to sudden outburst, rather of the older Gothic calibre, slow of incandescence, but capable under sufficient stimulus of being wrought up to a white heat, I had been inwardly

raging since Malgrade first came within scope
of my vision. I had refrained from violence,
though at desperate cost of self-repression, not
wishing to have it bruited abroad that Dolores
was the *teterrima causa.*

But one swift thought of the ruin he had so
nearly effected in my own case, joined to a
sight at the same moment of the woman's
bleeding face as it came between me and the
westering sun, precipitated such a wave of
wrath and desire for vengeance that I felt as if,
like Ugolino, I could have passed an eternity in
mangling the flesh of my foe.

Well was it said *Brevis insania furor est.*
What is it but madness when the whole
sensorium is merged in one reckless spasm of
blood-lust, careless—if but the hate-hunger be
appeased, the hate-thirst slaked—that fortune,
fair fame, life itself be spent in the effort,
lavishly as a child's toys of which he is
awearied ?

Powerless then, too, the disciplined will, the
instinctive inherited habit of prevision, to stand
against the dire half-animal transport. The
passion of Dolores, haughty and tameless as
was her spirit, seemed to pale before the

superior volume of mine, as with glaring eyes
I confronted him, her enemy and mine.

'Base dog, and son of a dog!' I said. 'How
dare you speak to a man that you have wronged
like me? You can beat a woman, you can lie
behind backs. Look at that woman's bleeding
face. Stand up to a *man*, you hound, and take
the punishment you deserve, for, by ——, you
shall have it now.'

A general misconception has gained credence
that evil-intentioned people decline to look
fixedly upon the countenances of the just or
other sections of humanity. This may not
infrequently occur; but the converse fact must
have repeatedly impressed itself upon even
the most superficial observer. Whatever his
evil doings, and they were comprehensively
numerous, man nor woman could ever say
Algernon Malgrade's bright blue eyes and soft
met them not fairly when he elected to deceive.
Clear were they, and burning with the fires of
hell when the demon within him was unchained;
but always unwavering, lowered neither to
friend nor foe.

As he stepped lightly forward with a mock-
ing smile on his lip, I watched their cruel light

deepen and glow, as might the gladiator's gaze in the old days of Rome, when the sword-play was before Cæsar, and the deadly inevitable stroke or thrust was impending.

In the matter of science as applied in the modern arena to boxing, no man on that great goldfield was his equal. But he had been lately leading an indolent dissipated life, while I had been taxing for the last few months, and therefore strengthening, every muscle and sinew in my whole frame.

Of these and other ideas I was dimly conscious as we went at each other with silent ferocity : on both sides the feeling of personal antagonism was too intense to suffer the intrusion of ordinary precaution.

From the first onset all notion of defence seemed to be abandoned, and the strange, curiously rare, sound made by the fall of heavy blows upon face and body, with our heaving breath, was the sole interruption for a space to the stillness of the sequestered spot.

I must have received a larger share of the first succession of blows that rained upon either form, but I felt or I heeded them not. I had iron muscles, a giant's strength in that hour, and, after fighting in to a 'half-arm rally,' which lasted for many seconds, I was less surprised than grimly triumphant when my adversary dropped senseless upon the turf, and lay without motion, prone and nerveless, as one dead.

Dolores had stood the while at a little distance watching the combat, her great dark eyes fixed upon us with an expression half fierce, half wondering, as though the contest, while ministering to her craving for revenge, was half painful from the mingled emotions which so inexplicably sway that most ancient and still unriddled sphinx of womanhood.

But when the man stirred not for a space, lying in an awkward position, as does a corpse, she slowly and unwillingly, yet as if drawn by a powerful influence, moved towards him, and then kneeling down by his side changed the position of his head, and loosened the kerchief carelessly knotted around his throat. As for me, I would not then have touched limb or feature to have saved his life, looking on him still with the loathing pitiless ire which the wounded serpent excites as we watch him writhing in the flames.

My evident feeling of abhorrence, ignorant

as she was of the deeper reason I had for revenge, commenced to produce a counterpoise of sympathy on her part. Gradually he recovered consciousness, and, sitting up, gazed at me with a look of malice so intense, so devilish, that I could have deemed it in my excited state to have issued from a corpse reanimated by a fiend from hell.

Shaking his fist, he moved his mouth and essayed to speak. No words came, though a gibbering horrible sound was produced. I saw Dolores, with a softened expression akin to pity, place her hand upon his face ; not till then did I observe with more curiosity than regret that the lower jaw was broken. My last left-handed blow, delivered with full force, had caught the lower face fair, at exactly the true distance, splintering the bone as if glass.

For the first time I felt partly avenged.

'You have shown yourself a man, Harry Pole,' said Dolores, as Malgrade fell over and apparently fainted, 'both in your pity and in your anger. I envy the woman who claims your love—the love of a good man. Once I had that treasure, but lured away by a villain, such a one as *he* (and she pointed to the prostrate man), I left home and happiness for ever—for ever. You had better return to your tent. I cannot abandon him in helplessness and pain, though in such a case he would not think of *me*. We part not this time, better for both if we did.'

Their cottage was at no great distance from the spot. When he recovered himself he would be able to walk there easily enough with her assistance. He was too well accustomed to feminine caprice to wonder at her change of humour. Doubtless they would effect a temporary reconciliation, as they had done many a time and often before.

It was late when I reached our camp. I crept to my bed and slept as well as the pain of my sorely-bruised body would allow.

My appearance on the next morning naturally created great and general astonishment. But I kept my own counsel. Of course, it was shrewdly guessed that I did not so disfigure myself. And the multiform though not dangerous injuries I had evidently received were not to be accounted for on any 'ran against a post' theory.

But I have before stated that in no com-

munity in the world is the anciently wise precept
of each man minding his own proper business
more strictly adhered to than upon a goldfield.
If somebody had 'rolled into me,' or *vice versâ*, it
was doubtless my own affair. If I had reasons
for not publishing the nature of the combat,
evidently a hardly contested one, why, well and
good also. It would come out in due time ;
and if it never did so, what matter ? So my
countenance was permitted gradually to recover
its normal contour and complexion without
exciting ill-bred remark or curiosity.

    .　　.　　.　　.　　.　　.

The great goldfield was still crowded and
surging, as it had been from its commencement, with human billows which foamed cease-
lessly around it—still ebbed and flowed the
human tide over its golden sands. For the
earth, pierced and torn and riddled in every
direction for miles upon miles, still gave to the
ceaseless toil of the excited and tireless crowd
gold dust and ingots in such profusion as might
have excited the envy of a gnome.

Some idea may be formed of the vast
quantity actually produced by a glance at the
official register of the period. It is there

recorded by Commissioner Blake that within two years not less than three hundred thousand ounces of gold were sent to the metropolis by the Government escort alone. Much was also taken to Sydney or Melbourne by miners who preferred the hazardous plan of carrying their own treasure. Making all due allowances, gold to the value of a million and a half sterling must have been reft from the forgotten subterranean river-beds of the Oxley during the two years that we spent there.

.    .    .    .    .    .

And now the weather of the spring I refer to came in exceptionally wet and stormy. For weeks heavy drenching rain soaked the forests, the plains, the low-lying flats, making lakelets and pools of standing water where but lately the dust rose in red or yellowish white clouds, and the tired eyes shrank from the refracted glare of the glittering quartz-strewn streets and the red massed mullock heaps.

The streams, filled to overflowing, ran foaming along their channels, or, raised above them by heavy rains amid the cloud-capped mountains at their sources, ran riot in devastating flood, sweeping away from the lower lands the cottage-

homes and crops of farmers, the flocks and
fences of the larger graziers, the dams and
water-races of the sluice-employing miner, while
every week brought news of deaths by drowning
in the dangerous fords of the unbridged streams.
Coach passengers, or the horsemen or ordinary
post traveller, the peripatetic labourer of the
colonies, all shared and suffered alike.

What was curious was that the winter
proper, which in Australia extends from June
to August, had been exceptionally dry and
fine. An occasional week of hard frost perhaps, with the thermometer down to 25°
Fahr., but on the whole glorious weather—
fresh, pure, invigorating, without tempest or
inclement weather of any kind.

But in September the weather changed with
the rapid unheralded suddenness of the Australian seasons. Sleet-storms and heavy-driving
gales of polar severity succeeded the bright
noons and cloudless morns of the midwinter
period.

Unprotected as our encampment was in the
essentials of substantial buildings, the change
of weather fell upon us like a Russian winter
campaign.

A change came over the aspect of the whole settlement. The tents and bark-covered buildings, blown down or soaked through and through, looked bedraggled and forlorn. The women and children suffered much, doubtless; for these last there was no play now outside of their homes, in which the narrow space precluded all but huddling and overcrowding for warmth and shelter.

The miners were now often hindered from their regular labour, and in the intervals, when the claims were 'off work,' might be seen grouped in or immediately around the bars of the hotels. These establishments did a roaring trade in hot grog, for the greater convenience of furnishing which ingeniously contrived receptacles of boiling water were kept simmering all day and half the night on the counters.

I was sitting with Bagstock at the camp, at which palatial residence we were not disinclined occasionally to spend an evening, when a miner came to the door and requested to see the Clerk of the Court upon very urgent business.

This was no doubt informal, the 'Govern-

ment time,' to which Bagstock was so fond of
referring, only lasting from 10 o'clock to 4 P.M.,
as in more settled communities. But of course
in real emergency no hard and fast line was
drawn.

'What d'ye want, my m-m-man?' said
Bagstock, looking at the drenched figure and
splashed garments of the messenger. 'Look
sharp! it's awfully c-c-cold.'

'I daresay it is,' said the man, looking down
at his steaming horse, the heaving sides of
which betokened the pace at which they had
travelled. 'I hadn't time to think about it. I
was sent to ask you to, if you'd come and marry
a party to-night.'

'Marry a p-p-party?' echoes the astonished
functionary. 'Couldn't they c-c-c-come to me?
C-c-can't they w-w-wait till m-m-morning?'

'They can't come, and if they wait till
morning it will be too late,' said the man
solemnly, a tall gaunt Forty - Niner, as the
Californian diggers were called who had been
at the first discovery.

'Where is it, th-th-then?' asked Bagstock.

'At the Gravel Pits,' said the messenger,
naming a diggings more than ten miles off, on

an exceptionally bad road, and with a dangerous
creek to cross.

'The Gravel Pits!' said Bagstock. 'The
G-g-g-gravel Pits, and on this sort of night!'
Here the wind howled afresh and the rain
poured down obliquely in swirls and eddies as
if bent on finding its way into every cranny
and corner by sideling intrusion. 'Why, I
w-wouldn't go there to-night for f-f-fifty
pounds!'

'I'll give you fifty pounds, half down,' said
the unknown, feeling in his pocket, 'if you'll go
at once; there's life and death in the cards.
What do you say?'

'Well,' said Bagstock, 'that alters the
c-c-case; done with you! I must muffle up, I
s-s-suppose. I'll order my horse. Pole, you've
got y-y-yours in the stable. C-c-come along
for c-c-company.'

In five minutes we were mounted and all
three riding as hard as we dared through the
splashing sheets and streams of various depths
that lay across our path in every way. Bagstock was not always painfully anxious about
his work, but when actually compelled to his
task there was no fault to be found with his

energy and capacity.    Our guide took the lead.
I never rode in a wilder night, rarely along a
rougher road.    The ceaseless rain had filled all
the minor water-courses, and every road-rut was
running like a rivulet for hundreds of yards
together.    We waded through sheets of water
or sand waist-deep in unexpected pools.    Best,
our horses were tried and good.    As for the
message-miner, he rode ahead, keeping straight
forward towards some unknown point, and his
wiry middle-sized mustang seemed to pass with
instinctive cleverness the uneven blind tracks,
dangerous to all horses not gifted with the
marvellous surefootedness of the bush - bred
Australian.

A two hours' ride landed us at the Gravel
Pits, a section of the great stream of the 'deep
leads' which formed the crowning glory of
the goldfield.    Wonderfully rich claims had
been met with here, of which some, from
the character and preponderance of the 'pay
gravel,' as our Californian friends termed it,
had gained their present name.

'Here's poor Jim's hut,' said our guide,
pulling up at length with a jerk that brought us
all almost on the haunches of his nag, 'and a

better mate never handled a pick. But his time's up. The confounded low fever has about settled him. The doctor says he can't last another day anyhow.'

' But you told me some one w-w-wanted to be m-m-m-m-*married*,' said Mr. Bagstock, quite aghast. ' I'm not the undertaker. Who's the bridegroom ? '

' Why, poor old Jim is,' said the miner, taking the saddle off his smoking hackney, and letting her go with a pair of hobbles and a large bell which he affixed to her neck while he was talking. ' But you go inside, both of you, gentlemen, and you'll see all about it.'

He pulled open the door of the hut as he spoke, and held it open for us to enter.

The sight was a singular one. On a rude bedstead near the fireplace, scrupulously clean, and warm with all the usual coverings, lay the wasting figure of a man, the unearthly brilliancy of whose eyes and the waxen hue of his features showed that he was in the last stage of fever. Such a sight was by no means new to us. In crowded mining camps, as in all armies in tent or field, typhoid fever and its allied diseases claim their toll with fearful and awful regularity.

Day after day, when the weather was hot
and humid in the late autumn, had we heard
the 'Dead March' in *Saul* pealing and rever-
berating through the forest, and listened to the
tramp of the long array of mourners.

But these terrible muster - rolls had long
ceased, and save in exceptional cases like the
present, when the Destroyer after being battled
with through long months had finally triumphed,
were beginning to be forgotten.

Another remarkable figure in the *tableau*
was that of a handsome girl, whose whole form
and face were plunged in deepest despairing
grief—heart-broken, apparently, with the traces
of undried tears on her cheeks.  She was leaning over the bed, dressed in such finery,
including a costly white silk dress, as would
have excited the envy of most women on the
field.  She was dressed in bridal array evidently,
a veil covering partly her long fair hair.  She
also wore heavy gold earrings, a brooch of the
same material, and a necklace of brilliants.  A
large bouquet of white roses and camellias,
supplied by no provincial horticulturist, lay on
the table near to her.

We at once took in the situation.  Both of

us knew the sick man by sight, as also by
reputation. He had come here with his mate
by way of California, where he had worked for
some years, but had originally come from
Australia, to which land he had at first
emigrated from his native country.

He rose with the utmost difficulty, holding
by a bar suspended above the bed, as we came
in, and fixed his glassy eyes upon us.

'Glad to see you, gentlemen!' he said, in a
thin reedy treble, which struck painfully on our
ears when we recalled the strong man who now
lay so feeble and childishly weak. 'I wasn't
sure as Mr. Bagstock 'ud come, the weather
bein' that bad. I was afeared I shouldn't be
able to make an honest woman of poor Bessy
there. I couldn't have rested in my grave if I
hadn't done it—nohow I couldn't. Don't take
on, girl. It wasn't altogether your fault or
altogether mine either, as things arn't square.'

'Oh, Jim!' cried out the girl passionately,
fastening her eyes upon him with the intense
devouring gaze of love mingled with despair,
'don't talk in that way. I'm glad and proud
enough to be made your wife; but I always
knew that it would be so some time, and I

trusted you, didn't I ? Hadn't we better wait till you get well ? '

' I'm not goin' to get well, Bess, and what ain't done this night 'll never be done,' said the sick man grimly. ' So let's lose no more time. Bill's here, as 'll be best man ; and they can't say as you haven't a wedding dress and all complete, even to the bo-kay.'

Here the sick man tried to smile, but the extreme weakness of the facial muscles prevented the attempt from becoming anything but a ghastly contortion.

# CHAPTER XXVII

Iᴛ was but too evident that the strength of the principal performer in this strange travesty of the festal marriage rite would not last out much beyond the time necessary for the registration, so Bagstock took down the names, ages, nationality, and religion of the parties with methodical accuracy. The while the sick man watched and listened with painful eagerness lest anything should be omitted which might be material to the validity of the contract.

The girl made a flickering effort to appear calm and collected and then relapsed into her previous expression of deepest gloom ; while— how piteous to look upon—the sick man tried to rouse her, and actually forced her with tremulous fingers to take the bouquet into hers, clay-cold and unresisting as they were.

'What's the meaning of all this ?' said I to

our guide, who sat carelessly watching the proceedings with rather a satisfied expression.

'Well, you see, poor old Jim here, his wife
—that's his first one—and he didn't hit it over
and above well, and many a year ago in
Victoria she made a bolt of it.   All the boys
tell me that it was her fault and not Jim's.'

'And so I suppose he takes up with this
pretty young woman when he came on to the
rush here, and they were not able to get
married before.'

'That's about the size of it, Mr. Pole.   This
gal, she was the daughter of one of the selectors
at Blue Gum Flats, and about two years ago she
and Jim made it up to be man and wife, like.
You   remember   what   an   upstanding   good-
looking chap he were.'

'Yes, indeed, he was.   It's a sad change to
see him like this.'

'Well, his time's up.   A man must go when
his time comes ; he ain't had a bad innings, but
he used to fret awful at times when he thought
as Bessy wasn't his wife.   Now it's all right,
and he'll die happy.'

'But how can he legally marry her if his
wife——'

'Bless your heart, why he only got the news of his wife's death last week, and the moment he heard of it he orders the wedding dress, and the earrings, the brooch, and the bo-kay all regular, and sends me for the Registrator directly they come by "coach-parcel."'

The strangely environed marriage ceremony concluded, the new-made bride hid her face in her hands and retired into the inner room. The dying man lay back for a few moments, the strain upon his faculties having apparently utterly exhausted his failing strength. Bill lit his pipe, and seating himself by the fire seemed lost in meditation.

We prepared for our homeward ride, our horses being only hung up to the nearest fence, a practice to which they were well accustomed.

Suddenly the sick man raised himself.

'Bill,' he said, in a husky weak voice, 'come here.'

'All right, Jim, old man,' said the other, knocking the ashes out of his pipe, 'what is it?'

'You don't want another ride into camp to-morrow, do you?'

'Well, not particular. I'm on the day-shift, too, and it's rather tidy work putting in them

setts.    The ground's none too good and won't
bear playin' with.'

'Well, as Mr. Bagstock's here, and this job's
over, he might as well do the other one, and
finish this register business right away.'

'What other business, Jim?' said his mate
in a low voice, while Bagstock looked from
one to the other as if the mysteries of the night
were never to cease.

'Why, you'll have to register my death,
won't you?' pursued the sick man, fixing his
unnaturally large fever-bright eyes upon us,
'and why not do it now?    I shall be as dead
a man by this time to-morrow as ever was
stretched, and wot's the use of dragging poor
Bill in and losing another shift in the claim?
He told Lovett yesterday to have the coffin
ready, so there's no call to waste a day over
that.'

'Good God!' said Mr. Bagstock, 'who ever
heard of s-s-such a thing, r-r-registering a man's
d-d-death when he's alive.'

'What's the odds?' queried the persistent
moribund wearily.    'It's twenty mile there and
back to the camp.    As for dying, I've seen too
many chaps go under with this blamed colonial

fever or typho not to know the stages. When
a man's like I've been all to-day he never sees
another sunset. So just fix it up, Mr. Bagstock, and oblige all parties, will ye ? '

Mr. Bagstock, during his short residence in
the colonies, and moreover at the diggings, had
rubbed off many of his British prejudices ; but
this request so transcended in its ghastly signi-
ficance all his previous experiences, so contra-
vened all his notions of the fitness of things,
that he was on the point of flatly refusing when
he caught the warning eye of the dying miner's
mate. He whispered—

' Don't cross him, sir, he was allays the most
obstinate cove out. It might do him a mischief
to be disappointed, like.'

The sick man had again relapsed into a
death-like stupor, but the strong calm spirit
again rallied the fainting flesh—trembling as it
seemed on the dread margin of eternity. He
read in the official's eyes his request was
granted, and then repeated for Bagstock's information, who took down the items in a large
official-looking paper ruled and marked in
spaces, the required details. It was soon
over.

'It's the biggest day's work I've done this weeks,' said the sick man. 'I'm thankful to you, Mr. Bagstock, and to you, Harry Pole, for coming with him this perishin' night and keeping us company, like. Poor Bess is Mrs. James Bellinger now, and no man nor woman on the field can throw it up to her as she ain't. I shall die happy, though I never ciphered it out as I was to die on my weddin' day. Goodnight and good-bye! for it's the long good-bye, I'm thinking, and no get away this time.'

We shook the wasted hand of the doomed man, said a natural word of kindly farewell, departed for the world of light and life and strength and pleasure, where in a few hours all beneath the sun would still be strong and beauteous in heaped-up prodigality, and left the lonely bark to push off in the dread and awful hush of midnight on the dark waters of the shoreless ocean of eternity.

The moon had arisen, and by her silver light we rode slowly and silently forth along the lonely road that led from the little mining hamlet to the gold city. Our thoughts were full of the strong brave soul which was passing away fearless and unshrinking from the dread

summons that was even now reverberating in
his ears, careful in that supreme hour but for
others, loyal in the very extremity of the weakness of the flesh to friendship and to love.

'I was t-t-told,' said Mr. Bagstock musingly,
after a protracted silence, 'that I should see
some s-s-strange people on the d-d-diggings.
There never w-w-was a truer word s-s-spoken.'

And he relapsed into a silence which lasted
till we reached the camp. At that citadel all
were still up, and unusual excitement prevailed.
A telegram had come up to Mr. Merlin at a
late hour which evidently was of importance ;
his manly brow was overclouded, and his utterances were more curt, not to say aggressive,
than ever.

'What's the matter with you, Merlin ?' said
Bright. 'Bilious as usual, or is there any news
about those confounded bushrangers that seem
to be always just out of reach, like crows when
a fellow has a gun ?'

'Read that!' said the inspector, throwing
over the modern messenger of fate. 'Isn't it
enough to make a man curse the day he was
born ? There, I've just sent away all my best
men, besides Sir Watkyn, and now I haven't a

tracker that could follow a working bullock over a ploughed field.'

Mr. Bright read out the telegram—

'Ben Wall, supposed to have stolen Grey Surrey out of Bowdler's stables last night, has been tracked through Forbes towards Jones's sheep station.  Horse has a broken hind shoe.'

'The best chance I've had since they've turned out; and to think that it should be upset by such a casual accident.  I was half a mind to keep the men yesterday.  I knew it was a wild-goose chase.  Well, sergeant, what is it?'

For that worthy officer, with cheerful visage, appeared in the doorway, and having duly saluted thus spoke—

'The men are back, sir, and Sir Watkyn the tracker with them.'

'Thank God for that!' said Merlin with unwonted piety.  'Is he sober?'

'Sober as a judge, sir.'

'How did they change route then without fresh orders?' said he sternly—for no deviation from the strictest discipline was suffered.

'They got a telegram from Sergeant Redmond about Ben Wall having been seen near

Forbes. They afterwards met a man in a certain place, after which Senior-constable Evans acted on his own responsibility. Here's a letter, sir.'

'By Jove! we have him then,' cried out Merlin, 'unless the devil gives him better cards than usual. Have the horses fed. Lock up that fellow, Sir Watkyn, and have the men ready to start in an hour.'

The sergeant saluted and withdrew.

'The luck is changed, and the red hazard is coming up again,' pursued Merlin, with a gambler's joyous exultation. 'I see it all plainly. We shall have Mr. Ben as safe as a dingo in a dog-trap.'

'How's that?' I said; 'there have been so many false alarms.'

'It's all right this time,' said the inspector, opening his revolver case. 'The reward is a large one, and our friend has been "given away" at last by one of his precious pals. The worst of it is that we shall have to watch all the rest of this cursed cold night around a deserted hut in the ranges, and with the cold I've got I'm as likely to be a dead man as Ben is next morning. However, *vogue la galère.*'

While divers plans in the council of war
were being discussed, Mr. Bright, after deep
thought, contributed a suggestion.

'I can't go with you myself, Merlin, though
I'd like to do it of all things, because it happens
to be our quarterly balance day to-morrow, and
though the General stands a good deal from
me, I don't think he'd stand that. But I'll tell
you what I'll do—I'll lend you my breechloader.'

'Sorry we're not to have the support of
your presence, my dear fellow,' said Merlin
with much politeness, 'but we're not going
duck-shooting.'

'Nonsense. I tell you I'm serious. I wish to
heaven I could have a steady pot at that fellow
Ben Wall or Frank Lardner after the rascally
way they took a sitting shot at us. But what I
mean is this——' here his manner assumed an
unwonted earnestness.

'Well, what is it? Unburden yourself of
this dark and dreadful secret.'

'Now, you listen to me, Merlin.' Here Mr.
Bright laid his hand upon the sub-inspector's
arm, and in a deeply impressive voice spoke as
follows: 'You take my advice—*use a smooth*

*bore and green cartridge* ; it's out and out the best business when you mean close shooting at anything under a hundred yards. Revolvers, I know by experience, are *most* uncertain, though, perhaps, as I should have been a dead man twice over if they had always been held straight, I oughtn't to complain.'

' Well, well, old fellow!' said Merlin, actually smiling and exhibiting a rare amiability, ' I don't know whether I won't take your advice for once. We've had such bad luck lately with this gang that I feel ready to do anything to change it.'

' I must say I can't congratulate you or your men on your success in stalking or shooting either,' said Blake ; 'the civilians are having quite the best of it.'

' How's that ? ' demanded the inspector fiercely, looking up from his weapons.

' Why, you know that Campbell of Goimbla shot Daly, and Keightly shot O'Rourke. Lardner's out of the colony apparently. Gilbert Hawke's flown away too, so if you want to make an imperishable name for yourself, you must come back with Ben Wall's scalp at your saddle-bow to-morrow.'

'D — n Ben Wall, and you too!' said
Merlin, roused to unusual fervour by these
taunts. 'Sergeant!' he roared, 'are the men
never going to mount? By —— I'll break
the senior constable if my orders are not better
carried out. There's no discipline, no decent
punctuality of any kind on this infernal goldfield. I wish the devil had flown away with
the first man that washed a dish of dirt on the
Turon. Bright, where's that gun?'

'Here it is; and half-a-dozen cartridges.'

'Two will be enough,' growled Merlin, grinding his teeth; 'if I miss that infernal scoundrel
after having to watch his damnable hiding-place
in such weather as this, I wish my arm may rot
to the shoulder-blade. Good-night.'

'Take me with you,' said I, 'I owe Master
Ben a turn, and this is as good a chance as I
shall get. May I go?'

'You may go to the devil—that is, with
pleasure, my dear boy,' with difficulty recovering his affability. 'But look alive and have
your horse brought out. But you're half
knocked up already.'

'I shall be all right when the shooting begins,'
I said.

The night was now intensely dark—'the moonbeams broke and deepest night came down upon the heath' — bitterly cold, wet under foot, wet overhead, as we left the camp without beat of drum.

Well clothed and warmly wrapped up as we were, after the first mile the frost seemed to strike through all to the very marrow. No sound was heard but the occasional jingle of stirrup-iron or bridle-bit, as the horses slipped and stumbled; indeed, more than one fell in the perilous, rough cross-country tracks we were compelled to follow. More than one of the troopers was well acquainted with the locality, and could have ridden it like William of Deloraine—of whom the Last Minstrel's Lay avers—

> ' Alike to him was time or tide,
> December's snow, or July's pride;
> Alike to him was tide or time,
> Moonless midnight, or matin prime.'

Still, between roaring torrents, abandoned shafts, black forest-arches where no ray of starlight penetrated, and dismal water-logged flats, where only the marsh-frogs made chorus and the night-owl hooted, we should, it appeared to me, have made but indifferent progress but for the aid and leadership of the black tracker, Sir Watkyn, whose sobriety had been so anxiously inquired into.

This distinguished heathen was certainly on this occasion 'the right man in the right place.' Being commanded to take the lead at starting by Mr. Merlin, and to look alive and keep a straight track, as if it were the easiest thing in the world, Sir Watkyn rammed the spurs into his charger, and rode as straight ' o'er moor and fell, through wood and wold,' as if he had a private understanding with the north star. Wonderful, indeed, is it that he and his kindred still possess this power, so often denied to the over-civilised individuals of the imperial race, of passing with unerring accuracy from point to point of the trackless wilderness, by night too even as by day.

Blindly and persistently we followed him, since better might not be. We rode in Indian file, the troopers and I in the rear, sleepy and over-fatigued, taking it for granted that we should reach some place or other eventually. It was, perhaps, hardest upon Merlin, whose cough, impossible of repression, sounded ever and anon in the most hollow churchyard-like manner as the icy dampness of the air irritated his bronchial passages. But no consideration could be extended to the personal circumstances of individuals, until the robber-gang was stamped out. To their extermination the Government of New South Wales was pledged, and no detail or exertion was omitted which gave hope of successful capture. Many a trooper, and not a few of the subalterns of the force, dated the commencement of fatal chest ailments to the ceaseless watches and night marches rendered necessary by the prevalence of robbery under arms in the terrible winter of 186—.

It was long past midnight, and for all I knew to the contrary we might have been heading straight for Sydney, when our sable guide reined up short on the top of a flint-bestrewn range, where the corrugated stems of the great ironbark trees stood black and columnar against the ashen sky, sombrely regular, as though they had been fashioned from the metal itself.

Merlin and the senior constable rode at once to his side. He pointed to a small open space below, dimly visible, as the heavens had

cleared since midnight, and the stars commenced to make the contrasts of earth and
sky faintly visible.

'You see um Sheep-station Flat,' he said,
pointing downwards, while his teeth chattered
like castanets with the cold.

'D—d if I do,' said Merlin; 'but what
then?'

'Sam Towney's hut long o' that flat, that
old lambing station. That fellow, Ben Wall,
sit down long a that one hut, then Sam bring
him tucker to-morrow morning.'

'We'll bring him something for breakfast too,
eh?' replied Merlin with grim humour. 'But
you're a sharp boy, Sir Watkyn, to bring us so
straight; sober to a fault, I see too. Well,
virtue must be rewarded. Give me that "tot"
that I see tied to your saddle.'

Even in the dim light I could see the swarth
face lighten up, with flash of eyes and teeth, as
Mr. Merlin produced a capacious flask of spirits,
from which he administered to the guide a
carefully graduated dram, handing the flask
also to the senior constable and me, partaking
moderately himself, and then sharing the re-
mainder among the men.

'Now, our plan is, Pole, to lie quiet and surround the place till daylight. Master Ben's horse must be tied up or hobbled near the hut. He can't have him in the house with him. When he comes out we *must* drop him, unless the devil, who certainly has befriended him hitherto, comes to his assistance in person.'

The necessary orders were briefly given. Merlin, myself, Sir Watkyn, and one trooper were to spread around the front of the hut, taking such cover as the place afforded. The senior constable and two other troopers were to take up their position at the rear. The horses were to be left where we stood, all tied up by their cavalry headstalls, with a couple of men, who *sotto voce* cursed their luck, to take charge of them.

Led onwards again by the swarth scout, who crept along sinuously adown the spur of the range, we silently and cautiously took up our positions within about fifty yards of a dismal, deserted - looking slab - hut with four sheets of bark off the roof and a chimney which was all awry. Immediately at the rear of the building was a thick scrub, one of those timber covers in which a desperate active man

on a good horse might foil even a band of
Comanche Indians, let alone ordinary police
troopers.

'S———t,' sibilated our guide, 'me see um
two horse, one fellow gray horse, one fellow
bay, like it short hobbles.'

'That'll do, very good boy, but hold your
row and lie down,' said Merlin.  'That's Mr.
Bowdler's Surrey ; the game's netted.  All we
have to do is to wait till he runs into the decoy.'

The black dropped on the earth, and straight-
way became invisible after the manner of his
kind, while we waited more or less impatiently
for the tardy dawn which was to rise for the last
time on the outlaw's career, or to add another
to the list of mortifying failures.

For myself, I had no great natural inclina-
tion to the trade of robber-hunting.  I could
not help feeling some qualms of pity for the
human quarry, who in the prime of early manhood was presently to be shot down like a beast
of prey, or if captured reserved only for an
ignominious death.  It needed all my recollection of the cold-blooded attempt upon the lives
as well as on the gold of others, in both of
which departments I had suffered loss and

injury almost unto death, to harden my spirit
to the proper pitch of pitiless resolution.

Wearily the hours passed.   Stiff and sore—
cold and well-nigh frozen was I—were we all.
We could hear every faint sound of the forest ;
the cry of the night-bird, the rustle of the phal-
angers and the smaller marsupials as they glided
through the wiry frozen grass or climbed the
clear stems of the eucalypti.

We could hear the ripple of the tiny brooklet,
its existence mainly due to the late extraordinary
rainfall.    Gradually, in spite of my watchful-
ness, a kind of drowsiness came stealing over me,
just as the first dim gray streaks of dawn were
visible in the east—the east that was so long of
becoming illumined with the day god's fateful ray.

Near me, however, at that moment an opossum commenced to make his curious half-chat-
tering, half-mournful sound.   This unseasonable
outcry became so persistent that both Merlin
and I, who were near each other in the night
watch, were effectually aroused.   Indeed, the
creature became so riotously and aggressively
noisy that I kept looking up first one and then
another of the white-stemmed gums that were
thinly scattered over the flat, having completely

banished the drowsy feeling which had commenced to steal over me.

Merlin also was apparently disturbed, for he
moved nearer to me and peevishly devoted the
obtrusive performer to the infernal deities. As
if the creature comprehended the uncompli-
mentary terms in which he had been referred
to, the noise suddenly ceased; and as the
sound died away I saw by Merlin's sudden
alteration of attitude that something had at-
tracted his attention.

I looked towards the hut. Midway between
it and the trees behind which we stood came a
man walking slowly and heedfully, as if seeking
for something near and well known which had
not yet come within his sphere of vision. His
dress, which was certainly of a dull grayish
material, with a poncho over all, was so
thoroughly in harmony with the neutral tints of
the sky, herbage, and the struggling light, that
he had actually quitted the hut and approached
our position unnoticed.

But for our being accidentally aroused by the
opossum, it is far from improbable that he would
have passed our section of the cordon unchallenged.

# CHAPTER XXVIII

HE was evidently searching for the gray horse which we had seen hobbled, and to secure which he carried a bridle in his left hand. He came unsuspiciously forward till within about thirty yards of our post. Then Merlin, stalking forward from behind his tree, cried 'Stand! in the Queen's name!' in a voice which sounded strangely loud and incongruous amid the hushed solitudes in the chill, gray, ghostly dawn. At the same instant, from beside the tree that had apparently sheltered the hilarious opossum, sprang the black tracker, uttering a yell which made the forest ring to its farthest extent.

Ben Wall, for it was he, showed no surprise ; he had carried his life in his hand too long, doubtless had foreseen precisely this description of *réveille* far too often, to betray astonishment when the fated hour arrived.

Dropping the bridle, he faced round upon Merlin with wonderfully instinctive quickness, firing one barrel of his revolver with apparently the same movement of his arm, and giving Sir Watkyn the benefit of a second shot with the slightest change of aim. That agile son of the forest leaped high at the report, but whether from the result of the shot, or from natural elasticity of spirits, could not then be ascertained.

Mr. Merlin stood unmoved, but simultaneously with Wall's first shot he brought the breechloader to his shoulder and fired with deliberate aim. The robber threw up his arms with a convulsive motion, stood statue-like for an instant, during which every rifle and revolver in the party was emptied, and fell heavily upon his face — dead, and, but for the convulsive graspings of the tufted grass and autumn leaves that strewed the soil, motionless.

We walked over to the body, headed by the tracker, who rubbed his forearm with a vengeful expression of countenance. It had been more than grazed by the second bullet, and the red drops fell fast across the sable skin.

'Turn him over,' said Mr. Merlin. 'I

thought I should hold straight this time. There's the track of my green cartridge. Bright was not far wrong. It's too cold for the pistol at this hour of the morning, when there's no coffee to steady one's nerves.'

Merlin's aim had been true. The cartridge of heavy shot, hardly scattering at the short distance, had torn through the robber's breast like a grapeshot. Death must have been instantaneous. But every Snider and Colt in the party had left a mark. The corpse was riddled with bullet-wounds.

'Ha!' soliloquised Merlin, 'there lies Ben, stark and stiff, and not the worst of the gang either. I know a man and so do you, Pole, that better deserves to be there. However, wishing won't hang people, more's the pity sometimes, so let us get back to our horses and return to the camp. I wish to heaven these fellows would choose decent weather to be shot in. I feel a precious sight more like a dead man myself than a live one.'

We betook ourselves to where the horses had been left, having previously had the corpse of the bushranger carried into the deserted hut whence he had issued, there to abide until a vehicle could be sent for it. We caught the noble gray horse with his companion, and led him back to camp with us, whence he was restored to his owner, much to that gentleman's satisfaction. And ofttimes a merry girl, as in after days she felt his free elastic stride beneath her, as he stretched tireless over the forest turf, grew pale when told that this was the horse that carried the boldest bushranger of Lardner's gang on his death ride.

Of the final destiny of the gang mention may be made here. Nemesis, *pede claudo*, was in their case sufficiently effective in the long-run.

Gilbert Hawke, like Ben Wall, was surrounded and shot dead. O'Rourke and Daly had perished before by the hands of gentlemen whose houses they had attacked. Gunn was captured and hanged ; while Frank Lardner, the Robin Hood of the Australian outlaws, the planner and contriver of an evil which far outran the original conception, escaped to a neighbouring colony, and there, as a storekeeper on a distant goldfield, lived unsuspected a life of quasi-respectability.

Discovered, however, at length, he was apprehended with singular dexterity and boldness by a member of the detective force, and safely lodged in the gaol in Sydney, there to abide his trial.

Strange as it may seem—and this is no fiction, but sober historic fact, which can be authenticated by official records — there were technical legal difficulties in the way of full proof of his identity and complicity in the wilful murders and attempts thereat which had been committed by his band.

So, in vindication of the unsullied ermine of a British court of justice, the highway robber and homicide was spared the last penalty and adjudged but to undergo a lengthened sentence of imprisonment. Even this, at the expiration of a term of years, during which he had earned a good gaol character for propriety and subordination, was commuted. And in answer to a mistakenly merciful popular request, he who had attempted deliberate murder, had compassed robbery under arms, and had indirectly been the cause of the loss of the lives of scores of better men, was permitted to go free. He now breathes the free air of heaven, and walks unchallenged in another land; while the victims of his lawless greed, his recklessness, and his

evil example, lie rotting in premature or dis-
honoured graves.

.     .     .     .     .     .

The year 186— was evidently the commencement of a cycle of rainy seasons.  It
promised to be a year of flood and tempest.
But the more widely the windows of heaven
were opened, the weather keener, the blasts of
the spring-time which, with storm and inunda-
tion, seemed never willing to ripen into summer,
the more laden the alluvial levels of the Oxley
appeared to be with gold.

The yield continued to be enormous.  The
escorts were fabulous ; and save that the con-
tinuously severe weather necessitated heavier
payments for carriage, and through this increased rates of prices for all things that the
miner consumed, no other untoward result took
place.

No one particularly cared.  It was a land
where all were rich ; and men had lost the
memory of the relative values of commodities
dating from a period when money was scarce.

Olivera was perhaps the only man on the
goldfield who had not at one time or another
enjoyed his share of luck.  He did, indeed,

get sufficient of the root of all evil to live com-
fortably and pay all expenses.   But he never
seemed, somehow or other, to drop upon a
'golden hole,' though such might be above,
below, even within a few inches of his claim,
wherever he might chance to select it.

To him, however, a scholar, a traveller, above
all a philosopher, this persistent run of ill luck
made little or no apparent difference.   He was
always ready to explain the apparently inconsist-
ent behaviour of Providence in his particular case.

'No doubt,' he would observe, 'this total
absence of what ordinary people call success
would be dangerous to natures unaccustomed to
take a widely comprehensive group of occurrences.   For instance there's Ned Wright,
ex-pugilist, rowdy, blackleg, what not; he is
pursued by the police, and finally so much
harassed that in despair he attacks honest
work; he sinks with Tommy the Clock and
two mates hardly better than himself No. 2
shaft on the Pink Lead; and what is the result?
Why, that after getting down without rock or
water, they bottom in the best claim on the
whole lead, and make five thousand pounds a
man in less than three months!'

'It's dreadfully aggravating,' says the Major.
'How you stand it, old fellow, I can't think.'

'Stand it!' said Olivera, carefully filling his
pipe, 'what else is to be done? One can't
bring an action against Providence. _My_ idea
is that I'm being reserved for something better
than the Ned Wrights and Tommy the Clocks.'

'Harry Poles, Majors, Jack Bulders, and so
on,' said I, laughing.

'Well, of course, there are several ways of
looking at it. But after all (one's powers of
mind and body remaining unimpaired of course)
perhaps the longer the day of full fruition is
deferred the better,' pursued Mr. Olivera
musingly. 'Still I shall never give up mining
until I die ; and I'll take the long odds I land a
big thing before I drop.'

Not so calmly philosophical by any means
was our latest acquaintance and partner, Jack
Bulder. Whether it was the wet weather and
the unfriendly sky, or the absence of his brother,
before whom he always preserved a comparatively dignified demeanour, or both these things,
joined to the monotonous regularity of our
washings-up and the swelling of our credit
balance, which acted unfavourably upon his

nerves, but so it fell out that John Bulder became careless and unpunctual in returning to the claim from the hotel where he had now permanently taken up his quarters.

It began to be whispered about that Bulder of Greenstone Dyke was going crooked, queer in his talk at times, not so steady as he had been when he first 'come on the rush.' Gradually—for gossip, so rife in older communities where events are rare and of modest magnitude, is singularly slow and accurate on goldfields—the rumour became confirmed that John Bulder 'drank.'

And one unlucky morning, after a lengthy absence of our defaulting mate, a messenger came up from the Ballarat Hotel with a note from the landlord—a very decent fellow who had known him in that gold city—that Mr. Bulder had been 'on the burst' for several days, and that some one from the claim, he thought, ought to come down and look after him.

This was not good news. But neither was it unexpected. The Major had prophesied as much. We did not moralise on it. We knew exactly how much it meant; how much and no more.

A certain percentage of men on every goldfield, on every large cattle or sheep station, in
every country town in all the Australian
colonies, is subject to this morbid phase of
alcoholism—not by any means the weakest or
the worst members of society either.

The attitude of the public to the individual
who may thus transgress is much like that of
the gaoler in the *Old Curiosity Shop* on the
occasion of Kit's incarceration. He did not
reason much on the causes which led to parties
being committed to his keeping. Crime, as he
noticed it, was a variable and epidemic occurrence. Some had it, some hadn't, others mildly
—much like measles, smallpox, or scarlet fever.

Many men in all the localities and societies
referred to drink more than is good for them,
perhaps become intoxicated frequently. But a
man who has a regular burst, or 'goes on the
spree' habitually and periodically, is classed in
a different category. He is known both to
friends and foes to be one who, while having
the power to *refrain wholly* from intoxicating
liquor for a given and definite, often a protracted period, must have his full swing, must
yield in an uncontrolled state of utter abandon-

ment to the craving for a debauch when the temptation suffices, or when his hour has come.

For weeks, for days, for months, years even it may be, the restraining power is known to last. Then chance or continuous pressure breaks the bond of self-denial, and over the broken embankment the pent-up passion seeks its lowest level, sweeping away tumultuously in its flow all good intent and manly resolution.

For a space, days and nights are recklessly devoted to the delirium of drunkenness. Then, wonderful to relate, the possessed one is suddenly discovered clothed and in his right mind, though grievously shaken by the 'unclean spirit which had come out of him.' A new era of perfect sobriety, energy, and propriety then sets in.

The Major and I, therefore, much as if we had heard that Jack Bulder had sustained severe accidental injury, or otherwise come to grief, concluded to set out and see about him.

'I'm sorry he's broken out,' said the Major, 'the fellow's such a strong nature, for good or evil, that there's no saying what he may not say or do.'

'It doesn't matter what he says, that I know

of,' quoth I, 'and I don't see what he can do. However, we shall soon know all about it.'

When we arrived at the Ballarat Hotel, Mr. Hennessy the landlord met us with a very solemn face. He motioned us into the little room beside the bar which did duty as a snuggery and general office.

'Morning, Hennessy!' said the Major; 'what's up with Bulder; anything out of the common? All the same, Pole and I are obliged to you for sending us word.'

'Well, Major,' said our boniface, an extensively travelled man, who knew San Francisco, New York, and Panama better than the Australian capitals, 'I shouldn't have troubled about a little temp'ry kick-up, but I knew Jack at Ballarat, and it's worse than that.'

'How worse?' I inquired.

'In this way. He hasn't been sober for a fortnight, as one might say, till last Monday; since then he hasn't touched a drop but soft stuff and tea. The curus part of it is that he seems worse and worse. I'm afraid he's got the jumps coming on.'

'The jumps?' said I.

'Yes, the jim-jams, or whatever you make of 'em; the doctors call it D.T., or something of that kind.'

'Delirium tremens,' I returned, 'very likely, indeed. Is he noisy?'

'He 'asn't slep' for three nights, or stopped talking; keeps on gassin' about Ballarat, and the soldiers, that's why I sent for you. Some of the p'leece might tumble, you know.'

Here Mr. Hennessy looked extremely knowing.

'Well, suppose he does talk about Ballarat, who cares?' I said rather hotly, irritated with the show of concealment for which I saw no necessity. 'Suppose all the world knew he was there.'

'But not in Eureka stockade; not as Ballarat Jack, one of the principal leaders, for whom there is five hundred pounds reward offered, and who was strongly suspected of killing Captain Wayse.'

'Good God!' I said, 'you don't say so. I knew poor Wayse well, and used to dine at the mess with him in Melbourne. Do you think he was the man that shot him?'

'He's in there,' said the host in a low tone,

pointing to a room upstairs. 'You can hear
him talking and going on as soon as you
get to the head of the stairs. Here's the
key. I've locked the door at the other end
of the passage; you take it with you and go
up.'

We went quickly up the staircase, knowing
that it led to a large room on the first story,
which was used for masonic dinners, quadrille
parties, political meetings, and other purposes,
for which more than ordinary accommodation is
required. A dozen or more bedrooms were
situated on the other side of the corridor. Of
one of these Jack Bulder had permanently
possessed himself. And the other occupants
being absent on work or business, he had
at this time the suite pretty much to himself.

We could hardly imagine that he was alone,
for as we approached the door of the passage
at the head of the stairs we could hear a
voice denouncing, beseeching, defying, by
turns, as if in earnest conversation with some
one.

As we turned the lock in the door we heard
him call out, ' Stand ! not one foot farther ! I'll

shoot the first man that leaves the stockade.'
We paused for one moment, doubtful whether
he had arms, and then, smiling at our faint-
heartedness, pushed open the door and entered
the room.

It was a strange uncanny sight. Near the
centre of the room, to which he had withdrawn
himself, stood John Bulder, barefooted, in his
shirt and trousers, much in the same state of
apparel generally as he must have used when
superintending the washing of his ship's decks
in tropical seas.

His eyes, widely opened, were fixed with
dreadful intensity upon a corner of the room.
The expression of his face was utterly changed,
so thoroughly that ordinary acquaintances
might well have looked on him without recognition.

Then his eyes, dilated with horror, rested
upon us. His head moved unwillingly and
slowly away from the spot at which he had
been gazing as he cried aloud, in tones of un-
utterable anguish—

'Good God! they are almost touching him,
the blood from his breast drips over them!
Will they carry his blood about to follow me

through the world and torment me before my time?'

'What's the matter, old fellow?' said the Major. 'You're rather high-fed to-day. It doesn't do to play with D.T.'

'Who are you, and what authority have you to question me?' said the possessed, for such beyond doubt he seemed to be for the time, still turning back his head as if fascinated to the first point of his regard.

'Oh! you know us,' I said; 'it's only the Major and Harry Pole, your mates. You had better come home and have a good sleep.'

'How can I sleep?' he said in a quiet conversational tone, 'when *he* is there, night and day, by my bedside in the darkness, and here when I am awake and would leave him if I could.'

'Who is there?' I said, thinking to humour him, and knowing it to be an optical illusion, such as are common to those suffering from a disordered nervous system.

'*Who* is there?' he wailed forth, in tones that made me almost doubt his identity, so strangely awful were they with shuddering dread and despair. 'Who is there? who should it be but the man I killed at Ballarat stockade, while he was smiling in my face, Captain Wayse of the 80th. Don't you see the wound in his breast where my sword went through him, and the blood—the blood running still?'

Here the unhappy man threw himself down on his face as one who grovels in the dust, and drew his hands over his forehead as if to shut out the terrible sight.

'This looks serious,' said the Major. 'He may have been in the Ballarat riot, as a few men we both know here have been. But as to poor Wayse, who died of his wounds the next day, after pluckily leading his company when they stormed the stockade, he may have dreamt all about it.'

'I don't know that,' I said; 'it seems to have burned itself in on his brain in a way that another man's guilt could scarcely have reached. I met poor Wayse once. He knew the Leys well, and told me he had been shooting at a house close by the year before I went there.'

Here John Bulder raised himself on his

knees cautiously, and then turning away his head, sat down.

'Who spoke about the Leys?' he said in a hoarse whisper. '*He* was there too. I was a boy; he was little better—but a gentleman, just got his commission, and he seemed a little god to a country lout like me. How handsome he was, and jolly, kind to all and free with his money like a prince. Many a half-crown he gave me in the old days, for he used to take me out with him to carry the bag. Perhaps he'll forgive me yet before I die. Why can't I die? *I couldn't be worse in hell.*'

Here the wretched man sobbed and bewailed himself as if he had been the soft untravelled rustic his wanderings described.

After another interval he went on more collectedly, while we, seeing that unless he was placed in charge of the police for protection, nothing could be done with him, and doubtful of how great a proportion of truth was mixed up with these revelations, listened without remark.

'One day I had snared a hare; I used to poach a little—most of us boys did, as much for the sport as anything, and I was just taking her

out when the keeper collared me.  I was being
taken off to gaol—Lord! lord! how frightened
I was—when *he* came by, and never stopped
till he begged me off.  I could have followed
him over the world when he left the country.
He gave me a sovereign, and told me either to
'list or go to sea, that I was too mettlesome a
lad to make a ploughboy of.  I went to sea, he
went to his regiment, and now here am I, and
he is—there.  My God, my God!'

Here he leaped to his feet and commenced
walking up and down the room like a sailor on
a deck, always turning back at the same place
and markedly avoiding the corner where,
according to his delusion, the appearance still
abode.

'Why did I join the rioters at Ballarat?
Why did heaps of good men? because the
diggers were badly treated, hunted for their
licenses, chained up like dogs, knocked down
by bullies like Strongbow, and tyrannised over
by raw lads fresh from England.  I fought
Strongbow fair once, and beat him too.  He
was as strong as a bullock, but I was too
active.  He was a man, too; he wouldn't let
the troopers touch me.  There was a lot of

foreigners in it, too ; some good, some bad, and Americans.'

'Wasn't Yankee Jake there, too?' said I, by way of a distraction.

'He! Curse him, wherever he is! He was not an American at all, only a white-washed one. He was an Englishman, of a good family, too, turned out for villainy of some kind. He was a traitor, too. He sold us at Ballarat, or we should have had time to strengthen the stockade before the military came upon us. But that's not all he did.'

'Why, what else could he do?'

'What does a man like him do? work harm and misery all his days. I had a mate, a sailor-man, a real honest chap as ever pulled a rope or carried a tar-bucket. He'd come over in a West Indian ship after one of his voyages, married a Spanish-American girl, the prettiest young thing you ever saw. Poor Dick used fairly to worship her, and she seemed that fond of him she was never happy out of his sight. Dolores and he was like two children.'

'Dolores Lusada?' I said; 'did you know her in those days?'

'Know her, yes, and respected her, too, and

every man at the White Hills where we worked.
A neater, cheerier, better wife no man had, till
this Jake, with his wheedling ways and lies and
fine airs, flattered her out of her true and safe-
sailing course, and persuaded her to dowse her
flag and scud under bare poles before the wind
with him.'

'And what did her husband do?'

'Followed them everywhere to kill him.
Then came back and drank—drank till he
forgot all about his troubles. But when he did,
he was mad like me.' Here he laughed in an
unnatural ghastly manner. 'So they had to
lock him up for a few months. Then he came
out quite quiet, poor Dick, and went away, and
I never saw him again. But why should he
have gone mad? he never killed any one.'

'Nor you, either,' said the Major. 'Somebody has told you all this. You're only fancy-
ing these stories. Come along home with us
and tell Mrs. Yorke about it. She'll make you
some tea and you'll get a good sleep after it all,
and that will set you right.'

'I would come, for I am sure you're kind,'
he answered humbly, but as if he had never
seen us before; 'but he would come too, and in

a small place it would be too dreadful. His blood would run on the floor, too. You could not help standing in it. Ah-a——h !'

Here he again assumed an attitude and expression of fear and shuddering horror beyond all control.

END OF VOL. II

*Printed by* R. & R. CLARK, *Edinburgh.*